John Amos holds a PhD from the University of California at Berkeley and a JD from the Monterey College of Law. He has taught at university level for over 25 years in the fields of Middle Eastern Politics, Political Sociology, and Political Behaviour. His academic publications include two books, *Arab-Israeli Military-Political Relations: Arab Perceptions and the Politics of Escalation*, and *The Palestinian Resistance; Organization of a Nationalist Movement* as well as numerous articles in major academic journals. He has also edited *Gulf Security into the Eighties: Perceptual and Strategic Dimensions*. He has lived in the Middle East, most notably in Egypt, Lebanon, Libya, and Turkey. He currently practices law.

To the Egyptians, the students, my wife, and my daughters.

John Amos

THE STUDENT

AUSTIN MACAULEY PUBLISHERS™
LONDON • CAMBRIDGE • NEW YORK • SHARJAH

Copyright © John Amos 2022

The right of John Amos to be identified as author of this work has been asserted by the author in accordance with section 77 and 78 of the Copyright, Designs and Patents Act 1988.

All rights reserved. No part of this publication may be reproduced, stored in a retrieval system, or transmitted in any form or by any means, electronic, mechanical, photocopying, recording, or otherwise, without the prior permission of the publishers.

Any person who commits any unauthorised act in relation to this publication may be liable to criminal prosecution and civil claims for damages.

This is a work of fiction. Names, characters, businesses, places, events, locales, and incidents are either the products of the author's imagination or used in a fictitious manner. Any resemblance to actual persons, living or dead, or actual events is purely coincidental.

A CIP catalogue record for this title is available from the British Library.

ISBN 9781398442726 (Paperback)
ISBN 9781398442733 (ePub e-book)

www.austinmacauley.com

First Published 2022
Austin Macauley Publishers Ltd®
1 Canada Square
Canary Wharf
London
E14 5AA

He who drinks of the waters of the Nile is forever condemned to return.

   (Egyptian paraphrase of Herodotus)

The wise Qadi asked, "What is the nature of reality? If a tree falls in the forest and no one is there to see it fall, has the tree really fallen?"

The callow youth replied, "Who cares? As long as the tree has a good story."

This is such a story. Some of the events are real; some are imaginary. And some of the real events have been reworked by imagination. But, as with the tree, it is for the observer to determine the reality.

Prologue

Melisande had come to San Francisco for a brief visit, principally to announce her pregnancy. Tall and intelligent, my eldest daughter had her late Assyrian mother's beauty and energy but without her angst. I had met her mother, Jeannine, while I was teaching Middle East politics in a summer session years before. During a lecture, I made some comment about the ancient Assyrians having gone out of existence. After class, a very good-looking woman with grey eyes, whom I noticed always sat in the first row, directly opposite the podium, came up and said, "You're wrong; I'm an Assyrian, and we are still very much around."

Jeannine then invited me to meet her family, who had emigrated to Chicago from the Urmia region of Iraq. I accepted; after all, I'd never met a real live Assyrian before. I was especially intrigued by the description of her father, 'Big Al, the Assyrian'. Now, who could resist that? 'Big Al' turned out to be a Chicago lawyer, who was a very cultured and likeable man. I met the rest of the family and promptly learned their history. The modern Assyrians claimed descent from the ancients. They had been converted to Christianity by the apostle Thomas and were followers of the original (Nestorian) Church of the East. The Church of the East, along with its sister Christian churches, dominated the Middle East from North Africa to India from the first through the seventh centuries A.O. It adopted the Nestorian doctrine that Christ's two natures (human and divine) were fused. Its membership declined as Muslim forces conquered the Middle East; only small pockets of Christians were left by the twentieth century.

Jeannine's family, like most of the Assyrians in America, had fled the Armenian/Assyrian massacres: waves of ethnic cleansing that decimated both communities. The atrocities were unimaginably horrific; men were shot in batches after being forced to stand on the bodies of previous victims; others were cut to pieces joint by joint, starting with their fingertips; still others died with their throats half-slit to prolong the bleeding. The reports from the League of Nations make gruesome reading.

Jeannine's grandmother had survived the Assyrian death march of 1915 by walking through the desert holding one child by the hand with another strapped to her back. She later came to America via an arranged marriage (at a reduced dowry because she was short and rather plain). But then, heroes come in all sizes, and not all heroes are handsome.

Anyway, one thing then led to another. We got married, I learned to dance the 'shaykhani', and I picked up some Syriac. Syriac was a derivative of the older Aramaic, the language that Jesus spoke; it was the literary language of the Middle East from the fourth to the eighth centuries. I also listened to dusty single-sided recordings of Assyrian singers and was baptised Nestorian (full immersion, on a chilly morning, in a very cold tub of water). I met the patriarch (I shook his hand not knowing that I was supposed to kiss it – a faux pas; nobody's perfect). I even learned to eat harissa (the Assyrian equivalent of the Scottish haggis: not for the fainthearted), which was eaten at New Year's. Harissa was traditionally consumed with shots of whiskey New Year's morning. Sometimes the whiskey served as the 'hair of the dog'; on one New Year's Eve in Chicago, the Assyrian revellers boiled out of their hotel and tied up State Street with a line dance down its centre. I was second in the line behind the handkerchief-waving leader, cousin Raya, a retired belly dancer (I had never before seen or felt a woman's hips move like that) and hung on for dear life. Traffic stopped; police were called; the fire department arrived. The next morning was predictably ugly; much harissa and whiskey were required by the former celebrants.

I also became the father to two daughters.

Melisande was very proud of her heritage, and had, as an undergrad, majored in archaeology, with emphasis on Western Asiatic history. By the time she came to San Francisco, I was still teaching as an assistant professor at a local university. We were staying at the Marriott, and, after a brief breakfast, elected to celebrate by visiting the Egyptian exhibition at the de Young Museum. Melisande was eager to see the artefacts, since she now had a master's degree in Greco-Roman art and had spent some time in the digs at Pompeii. She had also worked with Egyptian archaeologist Zahi Hawass, a man famous for his controversial theories and wide-brimmed fedora hats and the role model for Indiana Jones.

We drove out through the park, found parking and walked to the museum entrance through a crowd of tourists in short sleeves and pastels basking in the warm summer day. Laughter and chatter and the sound of moving cars surrounded us. Along with others, we climbed the broad steps to the museum entrance. There, we were informed that the next tour would begin in an hour. Disappointed at the wait, we decided to kill time by visiting one of the modern-art exhibitions. As we ambled along, we talked about the way museums present artefact exhibitions (usually only partial collections, because of the insurance requirements). Melisande pointed out that early Egyptologists, including the Carter expedition, were little better than educated grave robbers because of their mishandling of artefacts and almost complete failure to document their context.

While we were talking, I thought I heard a faint sound echoing through the halls; a sound apart from the background tourist chatter: chink-a-chink, chink-chink; chink-a-chink, chink-chink, the unmistakable cadence of a belly dancer. Impossible, I said to myself, for a belly dancer to be in the august de Young. Nevertheless, as we walked, the sound grew. We finally reached an open balcony, and I saw the dancer on the floor below.

A small woman with long, dark hair, dangling earrings and multiple bracelets and scarves was performing, surrounded by laughing children. She wore a 'balady' (country) costume, a red flowing dress, and she was good, but I had seen better ones, Belly dancing originated in Egypt as a country dance; it was called 'country dancing' ('raqs baladi' in Arabic). The name 'belly dance' was coined after an 1860s' Orientalist painting that depicted a dancer hypnotising an audience of soldiers. Belly dancing was brought to America by promoter Sol Bloom in the 1880s and then popularised in the 1960s and 1970s by Serena Wilson, an unassuming Bronx housewife who became ten feet tall once she started moving.

Unfortunately, Serena died from a pulmonary embolism at age 73 while on the way to a performance (she was a heavy smoker). But as I watched from above, the dancer's sinuous arms, hypnotic hip sway and lithe movement reminded me of a scene in Cairo decades before. Then, I had looked down at a transvestite dancer, three storeys below, performing for four or five onlookers. The dancer, a young boy with his hair in braids, kohl-darkened eyelids and red-stained hands, wore a dark shirt and what looked to be a white skirt. I remembered thinking that I would never have expected to see this in modern Cairo: transvestite dancers were a phenomenon described by Edward Lane a hundred years before and had presumably passed out of existence. But there he was.

Then my memory went further, opening up.

Rosemary and I looked at each other; we had been summoned to Jones's apartment by police officers late one evening. Then we looked at Jones. He was lying on his back on the polished chevrons, arms and legs twisted at odd angles and puddles of blood all around. A small man, Jones looked even smaller in death. Beneath the collar of his white shirt, I could see a jagged gash and the pink end of a severed windpipe. On the floor next to him was an elegant green and brown Egyptian Mamluk carpet. This was odd, because Jones had a low opinion of Egyptian rugs: "They put them in the sun and run cars over them to make them look antique. Give me a good Persian any time."

The rest of the apartment was filled with miscellaneous furniture and loose stacks of papers, many with gold-embossed calligraphy and leather-bound books in Arabic. Against one wall was a large French bureau in exuberant Egyptian Rococo style: French-style furniture had been introduced to the Egyptian ruling class during the khedive period, as part of a Westernisation policy. Egyptian furniture makers had been enthusiastically turning out French reproductions since World War II. A severe green leather chair was in front. On the desk were more papers, several pens and a large brass-rimmed magnifying glass: tools of the Arabist. The two apartment windows were framed by dark-green curtains with gold Islamic designs running across their bottoms. The assemblage spoke volumes of scholarly endeavour.

Three Egyptian policemen stood over Jones. Two wore dark woollen uniforms that smelled faintly of stale sweat. They shifted uneasily in silence. The third, balding, with pale eyes and a pockmarked face, was dressed in a brown suit and was smoking an acrid Turkish cigarette. He made notes on a small pad and, looking sternly at us, fired questions: Did we know Jones? How long? Did we know his Nubian secretary, Saada? What did we know about her? Did she have any brothers? Did we know where she was?

In fact, I had known Jones for almost a year; Brinner had wangled my assignment to him in Cairo as advisor in an effort to improve my lacklustre linguistic performance. I was to meet with him once a week for a tutorial. "Jones is the jewel of the university's Middle East and Arabic Studies Department," Brinner had explained. "His scholarship is impeccable; he is ferociously famous. And he might even do you some good."

Jones's office was in one corner of the American University's Middle East Department. I trudged there once a week. On the way in, I always passed Saada sitting behind a small wooden desk. A pretty woman, with dark, aquiline features, she always smiled and waved me on. Even though I went by her every week, I never spoke more than a few words with her. Her English was good but with a faint accent, I couldn't place. She wore western dress and, though she was a Christian from the South (so I had been told), she wore a short hijab. Why, I never knew.

Jones's office was small and overflowing with shelves of books and papers. Jones would always be sitting behind a wooden table, reading and correcting some student's paper. He was usually dressed in a white shirt, dark slacks and ankle-high boots.

When I entered the first time, he had swivelled around, leaned back and peered at me as though he was looking at some strange being from another planet. Then he put down his reading glasses and said, "So you're the American. Why are you here?" He had a pronounced London accent, sometimes punctuated by the affected cough of an Oxford don. Answering his own question, he went on. "I'm told that your Arabic is beastly and that the administration is thinking of sending you home as a lost cause.

"Well, maybe we can remedy that."

He laid out a study schedule; I was to report each week for a question-and-answer session. No nonsense. "Arabic," he said, "is the language of God. Perfect in every respect." Ancient Arab grammarians, in a labour of love, had structured the grammar into Aristotelian categories of being. There were at least fourteen variations of any verb and five accusative cases, not to mention multiple subtle grammatical niceties that allowed expressions not possible in English. "Given all this," he finished, "nobody here in Egypt is going to put up with your mucking around with their beautiful language."

Over time, the sessions devolved into more relaxed exchanges, especially as I improved in Jones's opinion. At one point, Jones asked me why I didn't join the Sporting Club. "It's been in existence for at least a hundred years. Everybody who's anybody belongs. Lord Comer was a member; Allenby dropped in; even Lawrence himself joined. Nasser plotted Farouk's overthrow there. You should go; it's really quite lovely.

"Except on Saturdays, when the young Egyptian officers come. Then things get a little sticky."

Months later, he returned to his original question. "So, why are you in Cairo? You're not like the others. They're workaday academics. No, you're different. You're a Welshman like me. You're like Marius in *Fanny*, who was driven to sail to faraway places. It's the wanderlust; it's in the blood. The Scots went out to the Empire because they moved from the bottom in England to the upper class in India and elsewhere. Read your Kipling. But the Welsh were different; why on earth would Burton trudge through Africa looking for a river? Why would Lawrence spend part of his life in the Arabian Desert? Makes no sense to ordinary people. As for me, I may go back to England, but I'll come here to die. For me, Egypt is like the elephant's graveyard. And as for you, you're already cursed; you have already drunk of the waters of the Nile."

"And, by the way, are you still humping that Egyptian woman?" Taken aback, because I thought Samira and I had been remarkably discreet, I asked Jones how he knew. "Don't be so naïve." He laughed. "Everybody here knows about you. You're the first real-live American most Egyptians have ever seen, and they're very curious. Didn't you once tell me that they even knew what kind of watch you were wearing?" That was true; I had once been in the school library, checking out E.A. Wallis Budge's *Book of the Dead*, when one of the staff, a young woman, came up to me and asked if I liked my Omega. I had never seen her before. I said that I liked it very much and then wondered about the keenness of her perception, since I would never be able to discern that kind of detail about another person.

But the question remained for the rest of my time in Cairo: had I, as a Westerner, lost the ability to perceive social cues that non-Westerners can easily see? Has post- Enlightenment individualism come at the cost of interpersonal connections? Or more broadly, has Western rational social organisation cut the individual loose from most social support? Sounds simpleminded but is really not; Sociologist Max Weber once lamented that the spread of 'rational' social organisation came at the cost of losing the 'mystery' of life. The cost of the Faustian bargain may be a different sort of damnation than usually depicted; disenchantment is its own special hell.

But the Western sociological idealisation of traditional or communal society is overbroad. As I discovered very quickly, the dead hand of tradition is very heavy. It leads to honour killings and the suppression of women. The very complexity of social interactions in communal societies also provides multiple bases for discrimination. In Egypt, there was a colour line, not as rigid or vicious as in the Old South but still there and immediately obvious. In addition, there was discrimination based on tribal or ethnic origin, language, dialect and even accent. Professor Higgins would have been at home in Cairo.

While I was still in Berkeley, suffering death by a thousand Arabic verbal nouns, the morning's conversation turned to the subject of 'maids' ('khadama' in Arabic). I was asked to make a sentence using the word. I did: "The khadama went swimming in the pool on Saturday." The Egyptian instructor was visibly outraged.

"What you said is impossible, try again," she said.

"But that is a grammatically correct sentence," I objected.

"It is not correct." She snorted, "Khadamas never go swimming."

Jones went on, "You should be very careful about banging a local woman. Her relatives probably want vengeance. You're a prime candidate for an honour killing. I'm surprised that you're still alive. My guess is that someone high up is protecting you. The Egyptian government certainly does not want an international incident growing out of your murder." Then, "Well, enough of this, let's have a drink." Our sessions were usually scheduled in the late afternoon, and after a while ended with drinks.

Jones would drink scotch and for me, bourbon. Once, he had found a bottle of Old Crow and handed it over with a flourish and a grin. "I don't understand why you Americans name your whiskey after birds."

Afterwards, we would drive around Cairo in Jones's Fiat: a dark-blue car, like all the other Fiats in Cairo. Jones had named it 'Isabel' in honour of Burton's wife, who, he said, had put up with a lot: all the pornography translations, and that running off to weird places, and especially, all those duels. She had destroyed most of Burton's works after his death as being unfit for Victorian sensibilities. But she had entombed Burton in a splendid marble mausoleum all the same.

On one such occasion, we were returning from the City of the Dead, Cairo's Islamic cemetery, which was actually very much alive with hundreds of families living in it. We had walked down the alleyways lined with towering marble and granite tombs. Jones amused himself by rattling off the Arabic inscriptions; some of them, dating to the Tulunid dynasty, were over eight hundred years old. It was almost dark when we drove back, the setting sunlight slanting through the car's dust-streaked windshield.

Jones turned down a narrow side street that he said was a shortcut.

Suddenly, he slammed on the brakes. The car stopped and lurched, the front wheels sliding. "I've almost put us in the Nile," he remarked, peering through the grimy windshield. Indeed, the front wheels were over the edge of the embankment.

"I can't swim, and I don't like water," I said.

"Neither can I," he replied. "Drowning in the Nile is not a good end for bold adventurers. Even if we don't drown, there's always the possibility of a nice case of bilharzia, although I think the water here is too fast for the snails." He took another drink (we had taken the bottles with us). "Did you know that Saint Louis, the crusader, drowned outside of Tunis? He was knocked off his horse into a canal and his armour dragged him down."

After a swallow, I replied, "I thought he died of dysentery. The *Private Lives of the Saints* says he died in his bed." The car lurched again.

"That's the official line." Jones gestured with the bottle.

"Does that mean that if I drown, I'll be canonised?" I wondered aloud.

"Not unless you're the king of France." He gestured again, then added, "King of France or not, we can't just sit here. Now, please get out and push, while I try to back this thing up."

My reverie was abruptly interrupted. The man in the brown suit stared at us for a long moment. "So, you really don't know anything about this. No one knows anything about this," he muttered, almost to himself. Then, louder, "All right, you may go."

I
Move Over, T. E

TWA 847 settled lazily down over the city. I looked out the window. A checkerboard of brown and grey roofs appeared, punctuated by fingers of minarets reaching skyward. The city flowed beneath, slowly at first but faster and faster as the plane lowered. As the plane moved over the runway, antiaircraft gun emplacements streamed below, their crews were languid in the dugouts. Now came military vehicles of various types, parked at odd angles, then buildings with sandbagged entrances, accelerating and expanding in size as they passed underneath the plane, all reminders that we were entering a country at war. TWA 847 itself was hijacked several years later by Hezbollah terrorists, its passengers held at gun point for seventeen days; some of them beaten, one murdered. The hijacking contributed to TWA's collapse.

There were seven of us on board, some with wives. Later, in Cairo, we met two more.

We were in various PhD programs and had been selected to go abroad under the auspices of the Center for Arabic Studies Abroad, a consortium of universities headed by Berkeley and Harvard. The academic plan was to go through an intensive Arabic program at Berkeley and then spend a year in country. The original idea had been to go to either Marrakech or to Shemlan in Lebanon, where British intelligence officers were said to train. But the war intervened, and instead we were sent to the American University in Cairo. This was probably the result of a larger arrangement by that university to avoid nationalisation and raised the possibly that we might be pawns in some arcane conduit between the U.S. and Egyptian governments.

The American University in Cairo was founded by Presbyterian missionaries in 1919 as an English-language university and prep school. Thanks to some heavyweight presidents, it developed into a major university, the academic equal of anything in the U.S. Its downtown campus, just off Tahrir Square, was noted for its Mamluk-revival architecture and the international brilliance of its faculty. After the 1967 war, it narrowly survived, partially due to a policy of absorbing the children of the Nasserist elite.

Later I was told that even Nasser's daughter, Mona, was a student. When I asked what she looked like, I was informed that she looked like 'Nasser with a long wig'. Not so. I once bumped into Mona in the school library; she was very pretty, very down-to-earth and did not look at all like Nasser in a long wig. (In a bizarre twist, Mona's later husband was charged with spying for the Israelis.)

All of us were also romanticists, each in his or her own way: some obviously motivated by Orientalist imagery, others by scholarly concerns and still others by darker impulses. Some motivations I could guess at, others I couldn't. All I did know was that every one of us was an avid reader of the *Alexandria Quartet*, of Durrell's dark Victorian prose, of his Joycean stream of consciousness, and of his wheels-within-wheels spy narrative. Before we left, each of us was asked if he or she wanted to withdraw because of the potential danger of going into a war zone without any backup. To a person, everyone seemed fully prepared to play *Quartet* games, including traveling to a country where, not six months before, mobs had roamed the streets shouting, "Kill the Americans." This did not look good, but it wasn't necessarily accurate; some reports of mobs may have been exaggerated. I was later told by an American businessman named McDonald, who had been there and seemed to know everything, that to his knowledge only one American, an oilman, had been killed. And even he wasn't killed by a mob; his throat was slit by the man who turned out to be my barber. After learning this, I was careful to tip the now sinister barber generously.

The Egyptian government had, in fact, gone out of its way to protect Westerners; most had been evacuated from the Ramses II station by air-conditioned train to Alexandria and thence by cruise ship to Pireaus. According to McDonald, the worst that happened to them was that they were reduced to drinking Cherry Heering when the ship's store ran out of whiskey. But that may have been the bourbon talking. However, Cairo was still a dangerous place, and there was rightful concern for our safety, since we would be the only Americans in Egypt, except for those remaining on the university staff, a skeleton crew at the embassy, some miscellaneous businessmen like McDonald and a few tourists.

Nevertheless, I still had to read through the *Quartet* in order to keep up with my colleagues. The *Quartet's* sweep was enormous, its detail simply spectacular. Durrell had obviously been in Egypt. The knowledge of the mundane details (like Owen Lattimore's description of tapeworm segments in Chinese outhouses) is what separates the amateur, relying on secondary sources, from the professional who has first-hand knowledge. And Durrell clearly had first-hand knowledge. Moreover, Durrell's handling of the narrative suggested that he knew a great deal more about the politics of the time than he let on. Some reviewers have suggested that Durrell was probably involved with British intelligence. A good guess, since all the other famous British figures that I knew about were similarly employed.

There were problems. Durrell's convoluted syntax made reading difficult (but then Durrell's ornate writing style perfectly expressed the ornate nature of Alexandrian upper-class society). The major characters were not especially attractive; Darley was a bumbler, Justine was edgy and spouted incomprehensible intellectualisms, Mountolive was a stuffed shirt, and the rest (with the possible exception of Leila Hosnani, but even she wrote turgid letters) were just unpleasantly odd.

Whether Durrell intended so or not, the *Quartet* was an unflattering picture of an expatriate community: very self-absorbed, very self-important and almost totally estranged from Egyptian society. Interestingly, there were no major Muslim Egyptian characters, although that may be by design, since the work was about the British occupation. The *Quartet's* Egyptian protagonists were Christians (Copts and Armenians) driven by the fear (rightly so) of being overwhelmed by a post-war Muslim Egypt. Nevertheless, the *Quartet* painted an accurate picture of the emigrant communities in Cairo and Alexandria during the British occupation. But the *Quartet* is more than an elegantly fictionalised history; it is a study of reality; in this case, the reality of the same series of events seen through the eyes of its various characters.

The identity issue presented another problem, one which plagued me throughout my stay in Cairo. The *Quartet* was written from a Western perspective, but that was much too simple and one-sided for someone, like me, who was supposed to be immersed in Egyptian culture. As an outsider, was I supposed to adhere to my American culture, or to relate to and adopt Egyptian culture? How to act when one is essentially operating outside the norms of both societies, unrestrained by either? Not an easy question. Was I to remain totally aloof, and imitate like the legendary British ambassador to Jordan who always dressed for diner in his black tie and tuxedo.

Or was I to go to the opposite extreme, like Saint John Philby, become Muslim and marry four wives? No matter what, the answer had all kinds of implications: The Knights Templar, who were ferocious defenders of Christendom, were roundly criticised by contemporaries for selling out Christianity by adopting 'Muslim dress'. Lord Cromer, who refused to make any concessions to Egyptian culture, was also roundly criticised as a bigot.

Not an easy situation for a sometime graduate student.

But there was an even more difficult problem: for Durrell, everything became sexualised. The *Quartet* treats four aspects of love, but its dominant theme is that, for its characters, everything is seen through the lens of sex. Sigmund Freud may have been right: the libido, if unconstrained by the superego (the personal introjection of societal norms) may drive history. The Egyptian society that I experienced percolated with suppressed sexuality. The institutionalised seclusion of women, by physical separation and by requiring them to cover themselves in public, produced a 'forbidden fruit' effect of intensifying sexual impulses. The word 'haram' means 'forbidden', and its derivative 'harim' (women's quarters) has the same connotation. But this prohibition coexists with the sexually arousing practice of belly dancing. The tension between these conflicting aspects of Egyptian culture has political ramifications. In the early 1950s, the Nasser government banned belly dancing. The popular backlash was so widespread that the government rescinded the ban (subject to the condition that the dancers 'modestly' not show their stomachs).

Other Middle Eastern countries banned belly dancing outright. Freud would have had a field day, as would have Alfred Kinsey. (Muslim culture, of course, is not the only culture that practises sexual suppression. The Victorians rigidly enforced a code of female 'modesty'.) For me the sense of acting outside the norms of either American or Egyptian society seemed to generate intense energy, most of it sexual. But this was later. And as I discovered, it was not my problem alone.

We had spent the summer and early fall in an off-campus location, drudging through both classical Arabic and colloquial Cairene (which to my ears had an almost Italian lilt). I was, as usual, at the bottom of the class, barely able to comprehend the Cairene dialect and totally bored because I had to look up word after word in Hans Wehr's Arabic-English Dictionary. That dictionary, a five-pound tome of Germanic learning (it also served as a doorstop), was my personal bane. Other students seemed able to use it with ease, but for me it was just an extra weight to carry around. But later, as it turned out, Hans Wehr was a formidable weapon capable of dispatching both humans and insects.

I had been seconded to Berkeley's Near Eastern Studies Department to fulfil the PhD language requirements of my home Political Science Department. My relations with the department were uneasy at best; most instructors appeared to view me as an outsider, not really a true linguist. In any event, late one afternoon, as I was escaping from a particularly dreary seminar in advanced Arabic grammar (something about the accusative of condition), a secretary blocked my path and said that professor Brinner wanted to see me at once. Brinner was the department chairman and would ordinarily have no reason for an urgent talk. This sounded bad. Nevertheless, I strode boldly down the hall, imitating a gladiator entering the Colosseum (Maximus is the name, and swordplay is my game).

When I got to the office, Brinner was all smiles. "We've selected you to study Arabic in the area. A little irregular, perhaps, but we were shorthanded, and you were the best we could do under the circumstances." Not exactly a glowing recommendation but good enough. Apparently, by some academic sleight-of- hand, he had gotten me selected to go to Cairo. "It will be total immersion," he continued, "because you'll be living on the economy and will have to use the language to get along. You'll leave at the end of this school year." Except for the total immersion part, it sounded wonderful.

Brinner, who resembled an aging Claude Rains and usually wore a light-coloured suit with matching tie, as befitted a department chairman, was by default my informal adviser. As chairman, he presided over what was easily the most fractious department in the university, a department divided into hostile Arab and Israeli camps. The curriculum, the course assignments and even the classroom locations were subject to partisan warfare; everything was fought to the death. However, he somehow managed to float above all this with a calm affability, at what personal cost, I did not know.

Even the most unassuming instructors were caught up in the battle. One of them, Professor Levi, an Israeli whose parents had fled Warsaw just before the Germans walled it off and who was the gentlest of men, once plaintively asked me why the Arab staff seemed to hate him. "I never did anything to them," he complained. "All we wanted to do was survive. What do these Arabs think, were we just supposed to die? Did they want us to walk smiling into the gas chambers? All I want to do is teach."

I told him that they considered all Israelis to be colonists who had viciously driven the native Palestinian population out with the blessing of a European-dominated U.N. And in any event, they considered his Arabic to be bogus; in their minds, he had just memorised the vocabulary and the grammar and mechanically put them together, without any understanding of the language. This, even though he spoke Hebrew, a sister language. I remember thinking that if that was their opinion of a pretty good linguist, what they thought of my efforts must be truly unprintable. But Levi's angst was palpable.

On the other hand, there was Professor Khoury, Lebanese and equally mild-mannered. Professor Khoury taught Arabic poetics, not exactly a politicised subject. Khoury was a man who wrote poetry himself and lived only to read and recite (impressively) pre-Islamic verse. I was never a fan of pre-Islamic poetry myself and dreaded having to translate it; the grammar was convoluted, and the words often had double and erotic meanings (for example, the Arabic word for 'mountain' could also mean a woman's breast), as in this Victorian translation of a poem by Imrul Qays:

> Stop, oh my friends, let us pause to weep over the remembrance of my beloved. Here was her abode on the edge of the sandy desert between Dakhool and Howmal.
>
> Thus, the tears flowed down my breast, remembering the days of love: The tears wetted even my sword-belt, so tender was my love.
>
> Behold how many pleasant days I have spent with fair women;
>
> Especially do I remember the day at the pool of Darat-i-Juljul.
>
> On that day I entered the howdah, the camel's howdah of Unayzah!
>
> And she protested, saying; "Woe to you, you will force me to travel on foot."
>
> She repulsed me, while the howdah was swaying with us.
>
> She said, "You are galling my camel, Oh Imru-ul-Quais, so dismount."

Imrul Qays was a sixth century Bedouin poet. He was the most famous of the pre-Islamic poets, a towering figure, and the beauty of his poetry was commented on by Muhammad himself. Even in English, the double meanings are evident. In Arabic, this gives the whole a kaleidoscopic effect of ever-changing imagery, of movement like the 'desert itself'. For me, even this short work was almost impossible to translate, and, in fact, there are multiple differing translations. Translations are difficult anyway; aside from the mechanical problems of word cognates and differing syntaxes, there is a whole range of emotive and experiential meaning that gets lost. Pre-Islamic poetry is meant to be recited aloud; when it is simply read, much of its power is missing. But when I translated 'qasidas' (poems) everything was lost, and instructors winced.

Lord Byron, however, would have identified with Imrul Qays.

Eroticism or not, I considered Professor Khoury to be akin to a Middle Eastern holy man: a man almost completely outside of contemporary politics. But not so. One morning, I had come to his office to talk about courses for the next semester. Unexpectedly, he opened his desk drawer and, his face contorted, pulled out PLO posters and literature and waved them at me. "Look," he said, "we have to recover our lost land, our lost honour. These Jews and Israelis act so superior; they call us WOGs (Worthy Oriental Gentlemen). I am daily humiliated. Worse, they bastardise our language and our heritage. We did nothing to them to deserve this. There were no Arab guards at Auschwitz. Here, take these."

Stunned, because I would never have expected such rage from a man whom I thought did not have a mean bone in his body, I took the papers. What a tragedy.

Actually, the posters turned out to be useful. I had gotten a teaching assignment at the university extension on Market

Street in San Francisco and lectured learnedly on Middle East politics to a motley group of students on Thursday evenings. One evening at the end of class, several students came up to my desk, declared that they were Black Muslims and, menacingly, that they thought I was too pro-Israel (although I hadn't said a word about Palestine). Since I had brought the posters, intending to show them along with Israeli materials, I reached into the desk drawer and pulled the lot out. Doing my best imitation of an Uncle Sam recruiting poster, I announced loudly that I was really a PLO recruiter, pointed my forefinger at them and declared that the PLO wanted them.

One of the other students who had also remained, an older, professional mercenary (between assignments) who cleaned his nails with a Bowie knife, just laughed. The group fled, and I drove back to Berkeley and had a couple of stiff drinks.

As if this were not enough, the department itself was embroiled in controversy with the university's library staff. One of its faculty, a professor of Assyrian studies, had checked out so many books that he had to climb through a window to enter his office. (The Near Eastern Studies Department was relegated to the basement of Barrows Hall.) His library card was cancelled. The groundskeepers were complaining about damage to the shrubbery. The library furiously demanded that the books be returned, or the staff would forcefully remove them. Moreover, the whole department might be banned from using the library. Brinner, as the department's commanding general, had refused to let librarians enter and had ordered the department's building locked. Temporarily casting aside their differences, the department faculty joined ranks against this outrageous attack on academic freedom.

I had passed by the offending office and since the door was, at that time, at least partially open, had looked in. The place was littered with books: in piles on the floor, stacked on a desk, falling off chairs – every square inch was covered with books. On one wall was a large poster depicting a winged Assyrian Bull. Perched on the books were Assyrian fertility statuettes: eight-inch-tall clay female bodies with parrot-like heads. Scattered around were Mesopotamian cylinder seals and clay vessels of different sizes and even some Babylonian glazed figurines. It was a collection worthy of any museum.

I had never met the professor before, but I did meet his implacable foe, the head librarian. As I was entering the library stacks one evening, he accosted me. He had seen my faculty stack pass, issued by the Middle East Studies Department and assumed (correctly) that I was 'one of them'. A tall, thin man, with unkempt white hair and oversized white mutton chops, he was every inch the head librarian. "Why," he demanded, mutton chops quivering, "are you people in THAT department so disrespectful to this library? Don't you know this is one of the world's greatest libraries? We are the equal of Harvard, of the Bodleian itself. Yet you steal our books and lock us out. For shame! I have asked the university president to allow me to stop all of you from entering this library." I mumbled some excuse about being only a teaching assistant and escaped into the stacks, up the wrought-iron stairs to the seventh-floor Ottoman and Western Asiatic collections, where I could dodge anybody in that labyrinth.

Eventually, a compromise was reached; half the books were returned, the window was closed, the bushes repaired, the card restored, and the office door reopened. About that time, I did meet the infamous professor: stoop-shouldered and slightly bald, with an innocuous smile and, ominously, carrying even more books. He seemed singularly unprepossessing to have caused such a rhubarb.

During all this, I had attended Brinner's classes on Islamic theology, meticulously researched and professionally delivered. His grasp of the complex and often esoteric material was impressive, and I could easily see why he was appointed department chairman, was considered a leading scholar in his field and was founder and head of the Arabic Studies Abroad consortium.

Brinner and I had become friends in the three years I had laboured in his department, and he seemed to appreciate my efforts. I struggled through beginning and then advanced Arabic and Islamic theology and history. But I was the bane of the department's long-suffering instructors. In particular, I had studiously observed their foibles and sought to exploit them (often, I admit, with some modest success).

One semester, I was required to take a course in conversational Modern Standard Arabic. In practice, this meant Levantine Arabic. The course was taught by an Iraqi professor whose office was at the end of the hall, across from the men's room: a location that befitted the professor's official status as a mere lecturer. The professor's name was Mrs Kassim, and her course had been scheduled for eight in the morning. The office was tiny and stuffy, little more than an enlarged broom closet. There were three of us, me, another student and the professor. We sat knee to knee; it was awful. Not only was it hot but some of the Arabic guttural sounds required a breathiness that made bad breath deadly. Occasionally, we were interrupted by the toilets flushing. After what seemed an eternity, I discovered that Professor

Kassim had written a PhD dissertation on Akkadian agriculture.

Now, as far as I knew, the Akkadians were concerned with drought control and had developed very sophisticated techniques to deal with it. So, at every opportunity, I would encourage the professor to discuss her findings. She was, of course, proud to do so; but, as she cautioned, her findings were secret and, looking anxiously out the door window to make sure nobody was around, she would point to the dissertation. It was wrapped in heavy plastic and hidden on the top shelf of the bookcase. The parallel with Lawrence's study of Crusader fortifications in the Levant, used as a cover for mapping Turkish military installations, at once sprang to my mind. But no such luck; there was no desert intelligence officer here, just mild paranoia. Anyway, the ploy worked pretty well; it was good for tying up one class every other week. That, along with my policy of strategic lateness, made the semester bearable.

Once, Brinner had asked me to drive him to a lecture he was giving, since his wife, who usually drove, was unavailable. "Could I drive swiftly, if a sudden exit was necessary?" he had inquired.

"Yes, of course," I had replied. After all, as a young Air Force lieutenant, I had practised four-wheel drifts in a TR3, on eucalyptus-lined curves in eastern Libya, under the guidance of Juan Fangio. And it really wasn't my fault that the ambassador's horse reared up and threw him off when I geared down and the engine suddenly roared. The ambassador, of course, was infuriated, but he never could find the culprit; he even called me into his office and demanded to know which of my men had done this heinous deed. Unfortunately, I knew nothing.

When we arrived at the Oakland auditorium, I learned that Brinner's lecture topic was to be the Israeli-Palestinian conflict and understood why the wife couldn't drive. A very dangerous topic, indeed, since the audience looked to be about eighty percent Jewish. As I watched, Brinner went to the podium and delivered a dispassionate analysis: the roots of the Middle East conflict originated in British promises to sanction the territorial claims of all sides, many of these obviously conflicting. The British knew this, but they were faced with the problem of survival against the formidable military power of the Triple Alliance. They needed allies; recognition of territorial claims was the bargaining chip to get them. British policy was straightforward: survive first, then straighten everything out if possible.

As far as Palestine was concerned, things didn't look too difficult; there was a very small, mostly religious Jewish population. Promising them a 'National Home' seemed safe enough. There was no observable prospect of a mass Jewish influx. European Jews didn't look like they were about to immigrate; in fact, German Jews appeared to support the Kaiser. Czarist pogroms had not produced any appreciable population movement. If promising to back a Jewish National Home in Palestine would help to get the Americans to enter the coming war, the benefits clearly outweighed any anticipated costs.

However, it didn't work in Palestine. The growth of competing nationalisms and the rise of Nazi Germany couldn't have been foreseen. Historians, with the advantage of time and hindsight, have criticised British policymakers.

True, these men had their own biases, but they were acting on imperfect information and under severe time constraints. There was no way they could have anticipated the development of a full-blown totalitarian state with its policies of genocide and ethnic cleansing. The consequential destruction of World War II was too horrendous to be foreseen. In a grotesque irony of history, the Palestine conflict and all of its fallout may have been Hitler's last laugh.

During and after the war, both Jews and Palestinians suffered major traumas. On one hand, there was the Holocaust, the physical destruction of millions; and on the other, the Naqba, the disaster, the displacement of hundreds of thousands. These clearly were not morally or factually equal, but their traumatising effect on the respective communities was enormous, should not be underestimated, and made any solution incredibly difficult.

For example, Abba Eban had once proposed a Middle Eastern economic union, a pooling of resources that had the potential to raise the Middle East standard of living and make it the equal of Europe. But because Eban was the Israeli foreign minister, the plan never had a chance.

So far so good, I thought. Nobody will be able to lay a glove on him. But then I noticed that Brinner kept glancing toward me, watching where I was standing in the wings. The audience grew restive. The speech drew to a close. No questions. Some in the audience began moving toward the stage. Then a murmur, "There's an Arab here." And everyone looked around in consternation. In fact, there was an Arab, worse, a Palestinian. He turned out to be a professor of Pentecostal literature at a local seminary and was rather innocuous-looking at that. No matter. Taking advantage of the confusion, we escaped to the relative safety of Berkeley.

Since I had about six months before leaving, I started training immediately. To become physically prepared, I joined a local gym. The one I picked out advertised: 'Train with Milo, a Mr America'. Milo? Milo, the strongest man in antiquity? Did he keep a calf in the gym? Now, that sounded impressive. As it turned out, Milo really was impressive: almost as wide as he was tall and with biceps like calabashes. (I had always yearned for biceps like calabashes).

I toiled with the weights. I listened to heavy metal music and admired the pictures of weightlifting greats (my favourite was that of John Grimek, the 'Monarch of Muscledom', who had 21-inch arms). I pumped iron three times a week and drank gallons of sauerkraut juice. Milo said that sauerkraut juice improved blood flow to the muscles and contained antioxidants. It probably protected against vampires as well.

I realised also that the Middle East was potentiality a dangerous place. I had been in Benghazi and then in Beirut during the American invasion, so I assumed that Egypt would be no less hostile. So I took up martial arts: judo, karate, aikido and even Tibetan yoga (for calmness under stress). All beautiful and sophisticated movement systems, but they required balance and control that did not come quickly.

Karate was taught by an instructor who never spoke but only demonstrated the moves, with grunts for emphasis. Judo was an exercise in formal drill. After bowing to Professor Kano's picture and then the 'tatami' (the judo mat), I practised throws over and over again.

This drill was then punctuated by the chaos of 'randori' (free play). As for aikido, I never could get the hang of its 'crack the whip' technique, although the throws were truly impressive. For months, I punched thunderously (and practised Bruce Lee chicken squawks), did knuckle push-ups (they really hurt, but then the pain demonstrated my manliness) and practised foot sweeps and hip throws. There is nothing so satisfying as the jar when your opponent hits the floor after a good foot sweep. I suppose all this was good for my character, but it was awfully hard on the rest of me.

Ultimately, I trained with a mercenary that was temporarily between assignments. A hard-looking man with facial scars, his mantra was straightforward. "You must kill or disable your opponent with one blow or move; if you get into a fight, you will lose. Here, just grab this knife blade tightly in your right hand and punch me with your left. If you hold it tight enough, the blade won't slip," he instructed.

"Suppose it does?" I replied nervously.

"Don't worry," he assured me, "you're left-handed anyway."

For good measure, I attended fencing classes (a gentleman should know how to fence). And even though the gloves and masks smelled indescribably, I enjoyed the athleticism and elegance: thrusts and parries done to the silvery chink of clashing foils and punctuated by the bong of bell guards clanging together. A music unto itself. I lunged mightily, like Douglas Fairbanks in *The Prisoner of Zenda*, but Ronald Colman always won ('sorry, old man'). After a few sessions, the instructor transferred me to the fifteen-year-old class. I could sense Fairbanks's disappointment. Well, nobody's perfect; perhaps I should have trained with Basil Rathbone.

At night, I jogged on a darkened high school track, a track half-lit by moonlight and lined with eucalyptus waving in the breeze, a practice that became a lyric interlude. The rhythmic thrum of the pace, the gentle breeze in my face and the sound of owls hooting gave me a sense of well-being and tranquillity that I had never experienced before.

In the mornings, I would feel the satisfying muscle ache from a practice well done. Unfortunately, I was never any good at any of it; I lacked both balance and coordination and was much too slow. I ended up smelling like a combination of an old tatami and Tiger Balm (menthol ointment for bruises), being covered with bruises and bumps where the fifteen-year-olds had stabbed me (even through the padded jacket) and suffering from arthritic hands and knuckles.

Mentally, I prepared by watching James Bond films (Roger Moore was my favourite, suave and elegant; the others were too crude). I supplemented Bond with a diet of old Alexander Korda epics: *The Four Feathers* was the best, especially in its depiction of the Battle of Omdurman, where seven thousand British soldiers took on fifty-five thousand dervishes. I relished the scene, even though I knew that the film's portrayal of the British victory was overdone.

Korda's version focussed on the final disastrous dervish charge. Filmmakers of the '30s and '40s tended to overstate Victorian military prowess. It was easy for the British to look good at Omdurman since they had repeating rifles, gatling guns, artillery and naval guns, and the Mahdi's forces did not. The actual battle was more complex and much more closely run. Dervish soldiers were more athletic and probably braver, considering the firepower differential they faced. Dervish commanders were tactically sophisticated and outmanoeuvred Kitchener's forces several times.

Churchill, who was there as a reporter, noted that at one point the 21st (Bengal) Lancers, with banners streaming, rumbled toward the Mahdi's lines, their lance tips low, aimed at the enemy's crotches and immediately galloped into a dervish ambush. As Churchill watched, two thousand dervishes materialised from the sand and (literally) cut down one quarter of the Lancers. The melee lasted less than 120 seconds by Churchill's stopwatch. Only an overwhelming infantry and artillery fire saved the remainder of the Lancers.

Many months after I arrived in Egypt, during a cruise up the Nile, I met some descendants of the Mahdi's men: black, with hawk-like features, very physically fit and dressed in white robes, they were clearly nobody to fool with. I could easily see how men like these could break the square at Abu Klea. The British were probably a lot luckier than they knew.

Nevertheless, I revelled in the exploits of Victorian heroes; and the Victorians (and Edwardians) loved heroes. Lytton Strachey's biography of eminent Victorians was immensely popular. Heroes like Richard Burton, Chinese Gordon and the later Edwardians T. E. Lawrence, Gertrude Bell, John Bagot Glubb and the like were household names. All of them legends in their time; all of them tremendously complex individuals.

My favourite was, of course, Lawrence; he was the man whose image as Lawrence of Arabia captured the imagination of just about everyone: writers, journalists and filmmakers. Lawrence was clearly the role model for Valentino's film *The Sheik*. I had read his books and also most of the books about him, and I even had originals of the Lowell Thomas articles. Lawrence was a complex and controversial figure: a figure surrounded by myths, some of his own making.

He was, by training, an archaeologist and had participated in the excavation of Carchemish with Leonard Woolley. But he, like most of the British academics who studied the Middle East, was recruited by British Intelligence. As a consequence, he had an influence on British policy that belied his official rank of colonel. He also had high social connections; he knew the Churchills, among others. In his books, he appeared to make outrageous claims. But later military archaeologists, looking at clusters of spent bullets, shell casings, and other debris, have concluded that most of the claims Lawrence made about his exploits were correct; and his theories of guerrilla strategy and tactics became the operational model for practitioners of what is now called 'asymmetrical warfare'.

Still, Lawrence was a man born in the wrong time, a man driven by hero worship, a man who, like Peter Pan, never grew up. But a man who acted outside of history; a man whose tortured persona still haunts us; a man aptly described by John Mack as 'a prince of our disorder'.

When I was in England, I had driven over the road from Clouds Hill to the spot where he died in 1935. Lawrence had driven his handmade Brough Superior motorcycle over that road in the morning and then shortly afterward had skidded off the road to avoid two young boys on bicycles. That was the official story. Unofficially, the version was that Lawrence had been assassinated when a black car had deliberately struck his motorcycle. At the time, Lawrence, a national hero, was allegedly pro-Hitler and an embarrassment to the British government.

I went over the asphalt road, barely over one lane wide and cambered in the middle, in a Triumph TR250 at about 80 mph. When I reached the curve where Lawrence went off the road, the answer seemed obvious: the road was rough, but more importantly, it was raised at the centre. Lawrence, on his high-powered motorcycle, would have been going at least 80 mph and probably faster, closer to 100 mph (he was known to drive at high speeds). A small bump, a patch of water, taking the line too high – anything, given the wrong camber – would have caused him to lose control in the curve, heading to the downhill straightaway. No need for bicyclists or conspiracy theories. I passed the accident scene at an easy 80 mph; a little farther on was a small cemetery where Lawrence was buried. I stopped. Someone had put fresh flowers on his grave.

I discovered and then joined, the Royal Central Asian Society. Headquartered in London, the Society was a who's who of overage imperialists and annually presented a Lawrence Memorial Medal. Society membership also required a second by a member. I wanted to be seconded by Glubb Pasha, nicknamed 'little father of no chin' by his troops and appropriately so, as near as I could tell from his photographs. (I actually saw him once at an airport and, yes, the photographs were correct.) General Glubb was the legendary creator of the Arab Legion. The Legion was the most ferocious fighting force in the Middle East in its time; the original hourglass shape of Israel was defined by positions held by the Legion. But instead, I got some ambassador, who graciously seconded this American upstart. Still, not bad for a beginner.

Later, on the way home from Cairo, I stopped by the Society. As I entered, I met Mrs Fitzsimmons. Actually, 'met' is the wrong word; she blocked my path like a female Cerberus. She was the Society's head secretary, who had arranged my membership application, and now she confronted me. She was an older woman, whose teeth seemed to be wired together. The first thing she said was, "Is it true that 'the' (read 'our') Canal is moving west?" Spoken like a true imperialist. Still, she was right due to currents and silting patterns the Canal was moving west. She then wanted to know whether Cairo had changed much since Cramer's time. I told her that I didn't know but that he was a fine man and the Egyptians missed him (they didn't).

Then, since I had enough of this parlay, I started sliding past her, but she started sliding sideways too. I slid again; she followed. I thought to myself, *why am I doing a slow version of the Castle Walk with this woman?* But actually, this was eminently in keeping with the ambiance of the place, and Vernon and Irene would have felt quite at home.
Fortunately, someone in another room called out her name, and she stopped sliding and left.

Having escaped from Fitzsimmons, I wandered through the Society's nee-Victorian rooms. It was like walking into a Korda set filled with heavy walnut tables, overstuffed leather Morris chairs, oriental rugs and velvet hangings. The digs were truly wonderful: battle flags on stands, frayed and burned at the edges; crossed sabers, pikes, and axes placed on the walls; glass display cases with medals. Photographs of ferocious- looking moustachioed men in splendid uniforms were everywhere. This was the mother lode itself.

Awestruck, I admired the full-length portrait of Lawrence and then wondered at the gigantic ram's horns (the Society's logo) on the wall. The giant ram, it should be noted, had been felled with one pistol shot by a Society member, who boldly stood up to its charge. Among the many portraits was that of another member assigned to the mission in Waziristan (northern Afghanistan). Known as 'Winkie' to his friends, this gentleman, like Johnny Appleseed, had spent his tour of duty planting apple trees. That is, when he wasn't busy putting down unruly Pushtu tribesmen.

However, physical and mental preparation was not the whole picture. There were medical concerns as well. Just in case, I spent some time in Berkeley's tropical medicine clinic getting as many shots as the staff would give me. Gamma globulin (for hepatitis B) was the worst; I couldn't sit for a week. I even asked for a yellow fever shot but was told that I was going to the wrong continent. "Look what happened to poor Arrowsmith," I complained but to no avail. Thanks to the clinic, I was able to take an arsenal of antibiotics with me, most of which I never had to use.

As it turned out, the British had eradicated malaria and sanitised the Cairo water system. We used to joke that Cairo drinking water had so much chlorine in it that it could walk around the room on its own. Drinking water outside Cairo was another matter. However, there was a solution: Coke. Coca-Cola, that ubiquitous American drink, was sold all over the Middle East. In fact, Coke could very well have been America's secret weapon in the war for men's minds, since it embodied everything American. In an odd twist, America was now subverting everyone else's vital fluids. General Ripper (of *Doctor Strangelove* fame) would have been proud. Subversion aside, drinking Coke was the perfect alternative to suspect drinking water, because the water in Coke was boiled as part of its recipe.

Fortunately, I didn't need all that martial arts training; I was taller and heavier than most Egyptians. And most of the

Egyptians I encountered were friendly, and many were surprisingly positive toward America and Americans. And the ones that weren't friendly all seemed to be armed with wicked-looking knives, and I was not into grabbing knife blades. After my experience with viral anti-American hatred in Libya, I had expected much the same in Egypt, especially given the general anti-American propaganda from the Nasser regime.

But no, quite the reverse: America was clearly a topic of great interest. Occasionally, someone would ask me whether it was true that American streets were paved with gold, and my impression was that the questioner was usually serious. American cowboy movies were regularly shown, and I was told that John Wayne was a great favourite. As far as Egyptian movies went, I went only twice. As near as I could tell, Egyptian movies alternated between three-stooges-like comedies and lavish Islamic period pieces. The sound was usually deafening. Omar Sharif was the premier movie hero. Nevertheless, I even saw a couple of students at the university dressed in cowboy costumes, complete with Stetsons and chaps.

By and large, the Egyptians seemed capable of distinguishing between America, the country and the American government's perceived pro-Israeli policy, although they were clearly disapproving of that policy bias.

Moreover, the Egyptians were clearly able to laugh at themselves: a refreshing trait and one very much in contrast to the slightly pompous seriousness with which other Arabs whom I had met seemed to take themselves. For example, the 1967 war was a tremendous blow to the Egyptian self-identity, and yet there was this joke:

1st Egyptian:	I hear the Russians are sending some advanced tanks, especially designed for us.
2nd Egyptian:	Sounds wonderful, how so?
1st Egyptian:	Yes, they have six speeds backward.

Oddly enough, there were several times when I deliberately went out of my way to proclaim that I was an American. This was because I didn't want Egyptians to assume that I was a Russian. The Russians in Cairo were highly visible and intensely disliked. After I moved to Zamalek, I used to look out of the apartment's window and see Russian aircraft, silver with red markings, flying low over the city, landing at two-minute intervals, at Cairo West, the military airport. Usually, the Russians (I thought, deliberately) flew in on Sundays, when everyone was at home and could watch. In person, they were Russian-looking (like movie characters) and Russian-speaking; some even wore lightweight trench coats. They were clearly out of place. The Egyptians, as near as I could tell, despised them. The Russians were both cheap and rude.

A couple of times a week, I would eat breakfast at a local restaurant, two blocks from the university. Usually, I would have 'ful bil bed' (eggs with horse beans), not because I especially liked this combination but because I could pronounce it successfully.

Sometimes I switched to 'kosheri' (a mixture of beans, grains and noodles topped off by lots of pepper sauce) – blindingly hot but equally pronounceable. One morning, as I was munching on kosheri, with watery eyes, one of the waiters sidled up and pointed to a couple of blond, beefy-looking men seated nearby. Russians, by the look of them. In almost a whisper, he said, "We tried to poison them by putting ground glass in their food, like we did to Napoleon's troops. But it didn't work. They must have stomachs of iron." Delightful.

But I was surprised that he knew about that historical precedent, originally described by al-Jabarti in his very solid history of Napoleon in Egypt. (Al-Jabarti was available in comic-book form in Cairo bookstores.) I was even more surprised that the Egyptians would try the same tactics over a century and a half later. But then I realised that the waiter's comments were an 'insider's' view of the Napoleonic conquest: a view quite different from that of Western historians and, by extension, an unflattering view of Western intervention in the Middle East.

Nevertheless, when the time came for me to leave for Cairo, I was as ready as any Victorian or Edwardian hero; move over, T. E. and all the rest of you imperialists. I was more like Bond than Bond himself, and my tango was better. I was as good as any of the whole mob; that is, except for the Arabic part. As near as I could tell, all of the Victorians and Edwardians-Burton, Gordon, Lawrence, Bell and the lot were fiendish linguists and could conjugate fourteen verb forms at the drop of a hat. (I later met a modern version of these Englishmen at a convention: a disgusting little man with pink cheeks and flawless Arabic.) No matter. I consoled myself with the knowledge that Lord Cromer didn't know a word of Arabic or at least refused to speak it, and he managed to run Egypt for quite a while. Of course, he had an army of occupation to back him up.

Anyway, American energy and know-how would make up for any linguistic lacunae.

Besides, I came from a line of adventurers. The oldest was a Welshman named Carver who was a professional highwayman and apparently the bane of seventeenth-century travellers. Carver was noted for his strength and was said to have once carried off a thousand pounds of pipe. (I could never understand why.) The latest of these adventurers was my Aunt Mamie. She taught Greek and Latin in a local Evanston high school during most of the year. The first woman to graduate from Dennison University in classical studies, she was a fearsome advocate of women's rights. During the school year, she was every inch the classical don. But during the summer break, she was no longer the proper schoolteacher. She would tour the Mediterranean (as befitted a classical scholar) and visit famous archaeological sites. Photographs of her taken at the time of her travels show a prim woman with the stern look of a suffragette, brown hair in a bun, round granny glasses, a small straight-brimmed straw hat and a very, very large purse.

I once went into her office, a converted bedroom in my grandmother's house in Evanston. It was cluttered with Greek and Latin texts and archaeological artefacts. I picked up one, a limestone 'ushabti' (an Egyptian funerary figurine). "Auntie," I said, looking at its back, "this has museum markings." A fleeting image of her industriously picking the locks of display cases with long hairpins drifted by. She turned from where she was sitting in front of a small Biedermeier desk and smiled.

"Indeed. I once visited the Egyptian Museum in Cairo," she said.

"And these clay figurines?" I asked. "They look to be first-century Roman." She smiled again.

"They are from Pompeii. I once visited the excavations." I looked around and saw a small piece of white marble. I picked it up.

"And this piece of marble?" She looked concerned.

"Put that down, dearie. That's from the Parthenon."

II
Dorothy, We Have a Problem

TWA 847 landed bumpily and then taxied slowly to a low white building emblazoned with 'Cairo International Airport', in English and Arabic. Stairs were wheeled up, the door was opened, and we stepped out. There was a slight, chill wind. I stopped at the top of the gangway and looked out over the airport. It seemed to be empty; there were no planes parked where I could see them, nothing but a few empty baggage wagons. In the distance, I could make out the gun emplacements. It looked deserted; there was a curiously desolate air. A thin wind whistled in my ears.

The next thing that greeted me was the smell; not that it was obnoxious but that it was different. There was the obvious tar and jet-fuel smell, but there was also something new, something different and troubling that I couldn't readily identify: a curious, animal cue that I was in a strange place. Something had triggered a response in my medulla oblongata, the primitive 'reptile brain'. There was a signal below the level of consciousness that something was different, possibly dangerous. Even though I became accustomed to many different smells in Cairo, this subtle sense of peril, and the feeling that I always needed to be on alert, never went away.

The ten of us on the plane were:

Jack and his wife, he from an Eastern university and already proficient in Arabic and Turkish. A large man, Jack was affable and seemingly self-confident, but surprisingly enough had gripped armrests of his seat in panic when the plane shook as the wheels lowered. Jack and I had become good friends the summer before we left. After a long week of classes, we would adjourn to the Rathskeller and drink gallons of beer.

Jack was a historian and eager to get on scene; he ultimately became a respected scholar and wrote several books on Mamluk dynasties. In Cairo, the pressure of grinding study drew us in different directions. To be more accurate, I became jealous of Jack's easy ability to master Arabic; not only that but he could speak Turkish as well. Intolerable.

Mark and his wife. Tall and thin, Mark resembled a worried Peter O'Toole. He was a man withdrawn and edgy; his fingernails had been bitten down to stubs. I never knew much about him; he rarely talked outside of formal recitation in class. Rosemary, the gadabout of the group, once told me that she had gone to dinner at Mark's apartment and seen empty wine bottles everywhere. In class, he always fidgeted, although he was always prepared. Throughout our time in Cairo, I could never relate to Mark, even though he always seemed friendly enough.

Broome and his wife, Marianne, whom Broome for some reason insisted on calling Henrietta. Broome was an affable man, slightly balding with reddish-brown hair and a small pencil moustache. He was supposedly sent to CASA by the Treasury Department. Other than that, nobody knew anything about him, but he clearly was not an academic. Since he and I were together at the bottom of the class, we became friends in our shared misery. Neither of us could pronounce the Arabic consonant 'ayn', which required making a sound that started low in the larynx and then moved to both nasal cavities.

Impossible. After a particularly embarrassing day in class, Broome turned to me and mused, "Imagine the Tabernacle Choir all singing 'ayn' in unison; the sound would bring down the walls, like Joshua's trumpet." A true statement. While in Berkeley I never had any dealings with Marianne, which turned out to be an unfortunate mistake.

Rosemary was thirtyish, blonde, brown-eyed and slightly gawky, with an awkwardness that concealed a very clear mind. Of the group, she and I were the closest friends, and I respected her judgment. Since she and I both had telephones in Cairo, we would spend hours gossiping like teenagers. While the rest of us struggled with 'cultural shock', Rosemary seemed to blend in with a good-humoured ease. Unlike the other women, Rosemary managed to get dates, often – it appeared – with young Egyptian officers.

And she had a surprising intellectual breadth; I later discovered that Rosemary had memorised the *One Thousand and One Nights* (not the porn Burton edition) and could, when asked, recite the doings of Shahreyar and Shaherazade at length. And, as I found out to my chagrin, she was also a formidable backgammon player.

Nora, short, heavyset and dark was second-generation Lebanese, a woman who smiled and giggled and was clearly uneasy at the prospect of living in Egypt, even with the advantage of being a native speaker of Arabic. Nora and I got along pretty well. We discovered that we both liked Middle Eastern antiquities, and we used to compare ushabti figures bought at Cairo's many antique stores. She (like me) was delighted by pharaonic architecture and considered it to be the equal, if not the superior, to anything in the West. Years later, I met her at a University of Chicago conference; she was older, the black hair was turning grey, and she had become heavier. She said that she was now head of the Arabic Studies Department at an Illinois college and had three children.

Tia was tall, with straight golden hair reaching below her waist. In Cairo, she was a striking figure; traffic would literally stop when she crossed an intersection, as drivers gawked at this blonde goddess. The other women were sometimes assaulted by local crotch-grabbers. (In Italy, young men grab butts; in Cairo, they try for crotches, though I noticed that only Western-dressed women were targeted, never women wearing 'niqabs'.) But Tia was never approached; she was just too formidable.

She was also in many ways unreadable. No one knew much about her, and she approached every personal interaction with the wariness of someone who had suffered untold hurts. At one point, Rosemary had disapprovingly declared that Tia was a bad person who had had at least one abortion (unheard of in those days) and had two young children somewhere.

While we were in Egypt Tia usually dealt with me as though she had just stepped in something distasteful. And she was, for the most part, my nemesis. That is, with one exception. About three weeks before we were scheduled to leave, Tia, Rosemary and I decided to do the tourist thing and ride camels in front of the pyramids. Rosemary had successfully mounted and ridden. Tia was to be next. The guide helped her into the saddle, and for a moment, she sat still while Rosemary took a photograph. But then she slipped over the top of the saddle and fell with a scream. I was standing alongside, and Tia crashed onto me. Both of us rolled in the grit. I expected her to push off at once but not so. She stayed momentarily motionless in my arms, staring at me, before getting up. I had not realised that her eyes were so blue. After we returned to the U.S., I never saw her again. I still have the picture of her on the camel, taken just before she fell.

Finally, there was me, owlish in black horned-rim glasses (I imagined that the glasses gave me the Clark Kent look). I was linguistically inarticulate and clearly the dunce of the group: not perhaps Berkeley's best representative. Even so, the group seemed to approve of me; the men were friendly, and a certain comradery developed. The ladies seemed slightly amused, sometimes exasperated but always willing to put up with me. Nevertheless, I had the sense that I was regarded as someone who spoke very little, was hard to know, lacked basic social skills and was slightly edgy to boot. Perhaps I was more akin to the socially maladapted 'heroes' of the preceding era than I really cared to be.

We walked into the airport lounge through glass doors that were crisscrossed with brown tape and fronted with a low wall of sandbags. Again, I sensed a feeling of desolation. The lobby area was empty except for three or four clerks behind long counters. Dust covered the floor and counters. The emptiness echoed.

We were immediately rushed by a tall, thin man and a heavyset woman. The pair introduced themselves as Abdul Masih and Hoda; both were Copts. They grabbed and hugged us. Their greeting was animated, profuse, bordering on the hysterical. I got the fleeting impression of an undertone of despair, of the hope that our group represented the beginning of an American involvement, of a new Western occupation. Heavy stuff for a bunch of graduate students. Durrell's description of Armenian and Coptic fears and hopes seemed to be playing out in front of me. For once, I had the good sense not to discuss sectarian politics.

I knew a little about the Copts: that they had a number of monasteries in the Sinai, St Catherine's being the most famous, and that their tiles and other artistic artefacts had a distinct Byzantine appearance. The Copts were descendants of the original Egyptians; they spoke Coptic, a linguistic offshoot of the original pharaonic language. They were converted to Christianity by Saint Mark in the first century. From the sixth century onward, they were subjected to second-class status as 'dhimmis' (non-Muslims). Under the khedive and the British Mandate, they enjoyed a resurgence as part of the expatriate community favoured by the British (see Durrell).

They were the largest minority in Egypt: some 10 percent of the population, about nine million. Nasser's socialisation decrees destroyed Coptic small businesses, and the Nasser government overregulated Coptic institutions, to the point where even minor repairs to Coptic churches were subject to governmental restrictions. Individual Copts were subject to hate crimes, and Coptic businesses were regularly targeted by the Brethren. The Copts were a shadow community, living in an uneasy limbo and constant fear.

After a few months, I got to know both Abdul Masih and Hoda. Abdul Masih had been with the university for years and had become the chairman's right-hand man and chief troubles-hooter, which is why he was assigned to manage us. A taciturn man that rarely spoke more than a few words at a time, he was reticent to talk about himself. I did learn that he was married, was a devout Coptic Christian and had several children. Two of his children had died young, from measles, presumably due to lack of adequate medical care.

Hoda was a widow, with three or four children. Abdul Masih was her cousin and had gotten her a job as departmental secretary. She also had been assigned to shepherd us. In the mornings, I would pass by the departmental office on the way (slowly) to class. Through the open door, I could see Hoda at her desk, covered with papers, at the rear of the room. She always smiled and waved. Whenever any of us needed any kind of paperwork, Hoda would be the one to fill it out. I got the impression that she pretty much ran the department.

Although they were a targeted minority, the Copts were also very nationalistic and believers in Pharaonism: the notion that Coptic culture is the direct and pure descendant of the original pharaonic culture. Normally, the Copts I dealt with were very circumspect about their political views. But once, in an unguarded moment, Abdul Masih, his eyes blazing, declared that, "We Copts are the true Egyptians. We are the descendants of the pharaohs. The rest of these people are Arabs who came here with Omar." Apparently, the Copts (or at least Abdul Masih) also believed that they were superior to other Christians.

After I decided to move to Zamalek, Abdul Masih helped me look for a new apartment. We found a small one and looked around. Suddenly, Abdul Masih turned to the landlady, a short, worried-looking woman and said (with increasing emphasis), "Madame, your apartment is dirty. It is dirtier. It is the dirtiest!" Then, he looked at me, obviously pleased by his demonstration of Arabic syntax. I was surprised; the place seemed very clean. I had opened one of the kitchen drawers and even the stainless-steel utensils in it had been buffed to a bright finish. As we left, I asked Abdul Masih why the outburst. He said simply, "The woman was an Armenian; Armenians are dirty people."

But that was later: at the airport, Hoda, with a flourish, handed over a tray of what looked like sandwiches. I bit into one. Ugh, a mouthful of sand. "Welcome to the Middle East," I muttered under my breath, "this is going to be rougher than I expected; the whole place is full of sand, even the damn sandwiches." But, of course, that was not entirely true; the 'sand' turned out to be falafel (deep-fried chickpea or fava-bean paste), which ultimately became one of my favourite foods. (And now a fashionable health food in its own right).

But the 'ugh' is the important part and that brings me to Dorothy. In the film, *The Wizard of Oz*, Dorothy was transported (by air) from Kansas (in black and white) to Oz (in Technicolor). In Oz, Dorothy was forced to deal with a universe that was completely foreign, a place populated by beings she had never seen before and a world where even the laws of physics were suspended. Dorothy managed to adapt to all of this with good-humoured aplomb and ultimately exerted enough control over this outlandish environment to return home to (good old, predictable, black and white) Kansas. The colour change is important; it signifies alternate realities.

Baum's book is usually seen as a children's story, but it isn't; it deals with the very real problem of cultural adaptation, albeit in microcosm. Easy enough for Dorothy but not for the rest of us. We jokingly called it 'culture shock', but in reality, it wasn't fun and games.

Kalervo Oberg theorised that there were four stages of culture shock: the honeymoon, the frustration, the adjustment and the acceptance. An individual who experiences disorientation when immersed in another culture works through the four stages and comes out (about 12 months later) feeling at ease. This, of course, is a model: an abstraction of elements from reality that is designed to provide understanding.

Models should never be confused with their underlying reality; they are like digital representations of an analogue world. Oberg's stages may all be true intellectually, but on the ground, the personal issue for each of us was to what extent we were willing to go to retain our original identity in the face of a completely foreign culture. What behaviours were we willing to jettison, and which were of such fundamental importance, real or symbolic, that they must be kept at all costs?

Acculturation, which is what Oberg is really talking about, involves a restructuring of personal identity. It is not an accident that young children learn a foreign language and adopt a foreign culture faster and more completely than adults; their identities are less defined and therefore more easily changed. Eric Hoffer writes that individuals dealing with a changing environment experience a crisis of self-esteem; they perceive that they are constantly subject to tests, requirements to prove themselves.

Here, astonishingly enough, those of us that were not connected to the Middle East by birth seemed to have an easier time. The Arabic speakers, like Nora, whose parents had migrated from Lebanon, and Marianne, the Palestinian, seemed to be much more conflicted and angst-ridden. The angst may have had something to do with cultural false cognates, cultural norms that seem the same but are actually different. Or the Arabic speakers might have believed that they needed to prove their Arab bona fides. Or it could have been more straightforward; since they were from a different part of the Arab world, they just might have not liked Egypt and Egyptians.

In any event, Abdel Masih and Hoda vociferously pushed us out the doors and piled us into several waiting cabs. We were to be driven to the Garden City House, our temporary hotel, until permanent apartments were found.

The taxis drove through the outskirts of the city: blocks and blocks of nondescript brown buildings punctuated by occasional listless palm trees. There were very few people moving about, most of them in 'galabiyas' or 'niqabs', some in Western dress, others in Western-style jackets over galabiyas. All of them looked bent-over and tired. Then, we came to the centre of the city: Tahrir Square.

Tahrir Square was built in the late nineteenth century as part of a Khedival remodelling project to make Cairo into an Egyptian Paris. The name Tahrir (liberation) dates from 1919. The square was ground zero for demonstrations. It was also the site of the Islamic funerals for RCC (Revolutionary Command Council) members. When an RCC member died, a large rectangular tent, draped in black, would be built and thousands of mourners would pack the square. The square was a magnificent series of concentric architectural circles around a large fountain, but now the fountain was silent.

There were more brown buildings and more people, this time in Western dress, along with the 'galabiyas' and 'niqabs'. In front of building entrances were half walls of sandbags; the windows were taped. There were large graffiti of the eyes of Horus on the walls. The few cars, that looked to be blue Fiats, had painted blue headlights. Store windows were also painted blue. There was a giant billboard of Nasser wearing what looked to be a beehive on his head (actually, it was a traditional headdress). Although the image was technically Islamic, it portrayed Nasser as a pharaoh. The billboard and Nasser's visage commanded the square. Later, when I would pass it on my way to school, I could sense Nasser's dominant presence in Egypt as a modern pharaoh, and by extension, his political potency in the Arab world.

There was garbage everywhere. In the middle of the broad asphalted streets, there were piles of horse dung. Everything I saw radiated defeat and despair.

We turned down the corniche, along the Nile and headed to Garden City, the suburb built by the British and the hotel. During the British occupation, British architects had rebuilt parts of Cairo, and Garden City was one of them. The new suburb had intersecting comma-shaped streets. These were constructed in accord with the then current British theory of riot control. The idea was to create intersections where urban mobs could be blocked by a few police or troops, and the curved streets, bounded by buildings, would prevent the rioters from generating straight-ahead momentum. This theory contrasted with the French approach built into the older Khedival renovations, which followed Baron Haussmann's concepts: these called for wide, straight boulevards designed to allow troops to line up canons and disperse mobs with a 'whiff of grapeshot'.

The Garden City House was a dump, but after a while, it became our dump, and we frequently ate or partied there throughout our stay. It was also a lot cheaper than the Nile Hilton. We were pushed into its rundown lobby, complete with worn-out dark brown leather chairs and plastic tables and pictures of the pyramids: a sort of Egyptian version of an older, off-the-Strip, Las Vegas motel. But it had a commanding view of the Nile and of Gaza beyond. The owner came out to greet us. A tall, hawk-like man reminiscent of Ray Bolger's scarecrow, he was effusive in his self-praise and especially so about his decision not to install air conditioning: it was a mistake.

We went to our rooms. Mine was tastefully decorated in pink and green and smelled strongly of rancid Turkish tobacco smoke. As I stretched out on an iron-framed bed with a thin, very bumpy mattress, I cursed myself for getting into this mess. Hopefully, things would get better.

Two days later, at the first meeting of our group, held in the office of University President Bartlett (a high honour for graduate students), we were introduced to Leslie and Cohen. Leslie was very much the Bryn Mawr graduate, with all that implies. Her charm was infectious. After Rosemary, she was the person I talked to most.

On the other hand, Cohen was an enigma: a large man, dark and heavy-set, with a huge handlebar moustache. He had come with his wife, very pretty but shy, she never seemed to accompany Cohen and remained almost a recluse. I never learned much about Cohen except that he was an avid photographer (which later got him into all kinds of trouble with the suspicious Egyptian police), spoke Arabic well and had a large collection of pet snakes back in the States. I never understood why, when the Egyptian government issued visas, it made no objection to Cohen's but held up Nora's. Nevertheless, what I saw of him, I liked, and we took to drinking tamarind juice and brandy (a lethal combination) on Sunday mornings.

Bartlett had become university president a few years before our arrival. A tall, balding man, he was the very model of a university president: smooth talking and very political in his calculations. He greeted us politely, welcomed us to the 'university family' and hoped our stay 'would be a happy one'. He was also very athletic and played a lot of tennis. In the afternoons, I used to walk by the tennis courts on my way home from class. Bartlett would usually be playing doubles with other dignitaries. It was my impression that the doubles game was really a cover for some arcane political negotiations held away from possible listeners and protected by the surrounding chain link fence. Bartlett had an excellent backhand.

But the problem of what to give up and what to keep remained for all of us.

Living on the economy presented all kinds of problems, but first on the list was food. Think of it: in the U.S., you could go to the nearest supermarket and buy anything you needed at fixed prices and consistent quality. Not so in Cairo: everything (at least at the beginning) was negotiable and the quality uncertain. Aside from this, everything, even the most familiar meats, fruits and vegetables looked and tasted different. And everything seemed to be undersized, or undernourished or just semi-starved. In fact, Egyptian society as a whole seemed to lack enough protein or fat. I lost weight, even though I ate often enough.

The first day of grocery shopping was an eye-opener. The nearest market was in a cavernous, open-beam, warehouse-like structure. Its floors were crammed with little meat and vegetable stands, some partially covered with awnings. The noise was terrific; birds flew about in the rafters and the place smelled of vegetables. I wandered around for a while and then went over to the biggest meat counter. The long glass case was filled with whole chickens and chunks of meat and fish. It had a large, round goldfish bowl on top. The butcher was a beefy man with stubble, wearing a grey galabiya a white skullcap, and a bloody apron and holding a large cleaver. He didn't look especially friendly. I pointed to a chicken and, in halting Arabic, asked the price. He responded. Outrageous. I pointed to the price tag and said, "That's not what it says!" He seemed surprised and then grinned.

"How much do you want to pay, effendi?" I named a figure; he shook his head no. Ultimately, we arrived at a price, a price that remained fixed.

He then appointed himself my mentor and began directing me (with his cleaver) to other counters. Apparently, he was an important figure in the market, because the rest of the shopkeepers didn't give me any trouble. I had lucked out and gotten the vetting of Mr Big. He said, "If you want pork, the pork store is nearby, it's open only on Thursdays. But you'll have to go early, because all the Christians come and make a big line." I followed his directions.

And after a while I became a recognised customer and most of the haggling stopped. The butcher would wave and smile every time he saw me. Once, when I pointed at some strange, dark cutlets on the counter, he stuck out his tongue and gestured at it. I guessed, "You mean…" And stuck out my own tongue (I couldn't remember the Arabic word). He laughed and nodded. Of course, I didn't know whose tongue it was but that didn't matter. At least the food problem was under control.

Then there was the matter of coffee. As an American, I drank coffee, not tea, not anything else, just coffee and lots of it, especially in the morning. The Egyptians drank Turkish coffee (which originated in Yemen): a strong, dark coffee, unfiltered and usually served with large amounts of sugar; sometimes cardamom is added. It is a social drink, and there is considerable etiquette involved. However, in the morning, it doesn't do the job: the cups are too small, the caffeine jolt is too heavy; it leaves a bitter aftertaste, and the coffee grounds are a nuisance.

Alternatively, there was 'dallah' coffee. Dallah, or Arabic, coffee originated in the Arabian Peninsula. It is stronger than American coffee and heavily spiced. Like Turkish coffee, there can be an extensive serving etiquette, and the coffee is usually served in small bowls (a major Middle Eastern airline has a how-to video for Western businessmen). A 'dallah' is the traditional hourglass-shaped coffee pot. Dallahs come in all forms, from simple brass shapes to filigreed silver and gold artefacts signed by their makers and literally museum pieces. The 'dallah' is depicted as a watermark on some Middle Eastern currencies. Its lines are exotically distinct; in short, it is an artistic masterpiece masquerading as a coffee pot.

The serving pieces for both Turkish and 'dallah' coffee are art forms set in a social context. The care and attention to detail that artisans devoted to produce both coffee pots and cups or bowls is evidence of their role in social ceremonies. Great art is usually thought of as something to be looked at in a museum or as a tourist attraction. Not so, it is displayed in almost every functional utensil.

Anybody can see the jaw- dropping lines of a Bugatti, or the deco glamour of the Chrysler Building or the ornate magnificence of a four-hundred-year-old silver pattern. But consider a doorknob: in the late 1900s, the Aesthetic Movement promoted the proposition that everyone should live surrounded by beauty. This concept was embodied in (Eastlake-style) hardware: doorknobs, hinges, faceplates and drawer pulls were created with elegantly sculptured designs. Perhaps a vacuum cleaner? The lowly 1937 Electrolux tank-type vacuum cleaner is considered one of the finest representations of deco style; it is displayed in museums and rightly so. Its lines are as sleekly deco as those of locomotives portrayed on 1930s' travel posters.

Unfortunately, there are no studies as to whether using it uplifted the spirits of housewives (or househusbands).

Magnificent art and moving ceremony aside, I still wanted coffee and lots of it – fast, with no fuss, no muss. But that didn't prove easy. The open-air market where the Broomes and I shopped had bags of green coffee beans. That meant they had to be roasted (obviously, upper-class Egyptians would have their cooks do this). So, I fired up the oven early one morning and discovered that coffee beans are extremely greasy.

The kitchen promptly filled with heavy smoke. A strikeout.

Next, I asked Abdul Masih if there was any place that sold roasted coffee beans. He thought a moment, and then said yes; there was a coffee importer about ten 'midans' (traffic circles) away. I walked over and bought a couple of pounds. But they still had to be ground. I found a mallet under the sink and pounded away. Big mess. Besides, they had husks. I put the pile of more or less crushed beans on a plate, took it out the back landing and bounced the beans up and down. It worked; the lighter husks drifted off and landed on the wall of the (officially closed) American Embassy next door. Back to the kitchen, I made a filter from an *al-Ahram* page and poured filtered coffee, very sophisticated. Passable but too thin, and it tasted a little like newsprint. It served for a while.

But then, someone (it may have been Hoda) told me that there was a store, a little further away, that sold ground coffee. Perfect. I came, I saw, and it was true; there were bags of actual ground and roasted coffee. The millennium had come early. I bought several bags. As I was hurrying back to the apartment, like Caesar bearing gifts, I paid little attention to my surroundings. So little attention, in fact, that someone bumped into me and the pen in my breast pocket disappeared. (I admired the pickpocket's skill; the pen was worthless).

Traffic stopped and I stopped also. I heard an ugly burp just over my head. I turned; it was a camel. Now, I don't like camels; they smell bad, they make unpleasant sounds, and occasionally, they bite. I have successfully avoided them for years. But this camel was at the head of a long camel train, apparently from the Siwa Oasis.

Close to the Libyan border, the Siwa Oasis was isolated and populated by Berber tribes. A couple of nineteenth-century European explorers died in the desert attempting to reach it. The camel, and train, had stopped to avoid running me over. Out of the corner of my eye, I saw a camel driver gesturing frantically. I scuttled out of the way and then turned to watch. A line of thirty or so camels, their bells and harnesses ringing and clinking, moved majestically past. The drivers, in full Bedouin (Berber) gear, walked alongside, shouting commands. I stood there, in the middle of urban Cairo while a procession straight out of the *Arabian Nights* passed. My mind jumped to the wedding procession in *Kismet;* all that was needed was Vic Damone singing. The caravan went on, the traffic resumed, and I went back. The ground coffee worked; the coffee problem was solved and order was restored.

Silly, you say. Not really. Drinking cups of coffee in the morning was a decades-long behaviour pattern, a pattern that, in part, set the parameters of my existence. I was no more willing to give it up than the British Ambassador was willing to give up dressing for dinner. (Imagine, putting on tuxedo studs in the middle of a riot: that's chutzpah.)

Once the food and coffee problems were more or less solved, I could look to find other reminders of home: pets came to mind. I had tropical fish in Berkeley. But keeping them in Cairo seemed an overreach. Perhaps something simpler, a goldfish, for instance. The butcher had a goldfish, so they must have been available someplace. I asked around; no one, not even the redoubtable Hoda, knew where to find a goldfish. Hoda seemed to think my quest was amusing. "Why don't you get a crane?" she suggested. "Cranes are friendly, and there are hundreds of them in Egypt." She smiled and continued, "The ancient Egyptians had lots of them; they put them in hieroglyphs, and they mummified them."

I shot back, "I don't want a crane, real or mummified, and I think the Egyptians called them ibises. I've seen ibis mummies and they are disgusting. I want a goldfish, alive and not mummified!" The ancient Egyptians mummified fish as well. In fact, the ancients seem to have mummified everything. At that, a thought crossed my mind (I couldn't help myself). "Do you suppose the ancient mummy makers were unionised? Perhaps there were mummy boutiques? Mummy rentals? Mummy decor?" The possibilities were endless. Enough with the mummies. Clearly, the ancient Egyptians were getting to me. In any event, this conversation was going nowhere, so I started looking for a pet store.

Eventually, I found one. It was small and crowded with pet goods and smelled like dog food and unwashed animals. There were all kinds of domestic and exotic creatures in cages around the walls. In one of the cages, there was a small leopard; in others were large snakes. There were lots of cats; the ancient Egyptians kept, and worshipped, cats. It was said that there was an ancient Egyptian cat cult still existing somewhere in the Delta. Some of the ancient breeds, like the Mau and the Egyptian Valley Cat, survive and are sought after; the pet store had a couple of them. I thought long about buying one – imagine being able to take home a living piece of ancient Egypt – but upon reflection, the problems of keeping it alive in Cairo seemed insurmountable. It would have to be confined to a high-rise apartment, and there were no veterinaries. A cat was out.

But there were still no goldfish. I asked the owner of the pet store if he knew where any goldfish were to be found. He didn't. "But," he said, "let me show you this parrot; he speaks Arabic." The parrot, a large, green-and-red bird, settled onto my arm. It was surprisingly heavy, and its talons, which did not dig in, felt warm: a beautiful and friendly bird. And it did, indeed, speak Arabic.

However, the logistics of getting a large Egyptian parrot back to the U.S. seemed insurmountable. I could imagine approaching a gimlet-eyed immigration-control officer with a fluffy green parrot on my shoulder (like a modern Long John Silver), only to have the bird squawk out, 'Long live Nasser!' Bad idea; I declined. Then, the owner said, "Come here, I have something for your villa in Heliopolis." He threw open a small door at the back; there was a dark room packed with bright pink and red flamingos. "See, see," he said, "these would be perfect for you, effendi. For your villa in Maadi." I declined again and left the store in despair.

But then, it came to pass. Early one morning, having struggled through the coffee making, I went out of the kitchen to the small iron landing with iron fencing and iron steps leading to other floors. Sitting on the railing across from me was a very large bird. It looked to be a hawk and an unfriendly one at that. My mind raced (while I backed up slightly): Sinbad was carried off by a roc, which must have been a larger version of this bird. I waved at the bird; it ruffled and shuffled but did not move. It clearly intended to sit on the railing.

We glowered at each other, nose to beak; time languished. Finally, I gave up. "Okay, you can stay; now I suppose you're hungry. Sorry, I'm fresh out of Sinbads, but I do have some leftover 'kufta' (ground meat)." I brought some pieces out and carefully put them on the landing between us. The bird hopped down, ate the kufta and then fluttered back to the railing and sat motionless. "Hostile devil," I muttered to myself, then I went back into the kitchen.

Ultimately, Doris (I arbitrarily named the bird after an old, obnoxious girlfriend) and I developed a working relationship; in the morning, when I opened the kitchen door, she would be sitting on the railing. I could tell by the droppings that she had spent the night. She would stare at me, unmoving, until I brought breakfast out, then hop down, eat and flap back up. Sometimes, I thought I detected a beaky smile, although that might have been my overwrought imagination (after all, I was socialising with a bird). But having thought about it, I concluded that she was an excellent guard hawk. Who else in Cairo had a private Horus Hawk? No second-storey man in his right mind would have taken on that bird. Doris stayed a couple of months and then left, perhaps to search for Sindbad, perhaps to find the Calendar Prince.

But why all the fuss about simple things like food, coffee and goldfish? Living in a foreign country (not as a tourist, who is essentially in a protected bubble) means that you experience a constant stream of new and strange information. In formal terms, your cognitive screen is overwhelmed by environmental stimuli. And these stimuli have the weight of acceptance by the surrounding society. At some point, your self-image, your ego is threatened. To defend against this, you recreate what is familiar, essentially as a dike to set boundaries. A psychologist would call this a coping strategy, but that sounds too passive. It was an active attempt to alter a foreign environment to make it more palatable. Each of us did this in his or her own way.

For me, it meant recreating some simple, old, everyday living patterns, such as coffee drinking or maybe a pet and a few other behavioural sets. For others, especially the women, it was much more difficult; they had many more social and cultural problems to deal with than we men.

III
The Little Man Behind the Pyramids

At various times, each of us encountered individuals posing as friends of America and offering 'deals' – usually shady financial arrangements which, if carried out, would surely have resulted in arrest or expulsion or both. We could never be sure whether these individuals were just financially desperate, independent sociopaths or government provocateurs, and we referred to them all generically as 'the Little Man behind the Pyramids'. Usually, we could brush them off, but the incessant sense of being targeted, the constant wariness, drained us. It lessened over time as we gradually became immersed in the surrounding society, but it never completely left us. 'Wheeling and dealing' was just part of the give-and-take of life in Cairo.

One morning, about two weeks in, as I was trudging to the university from my newly rented apartment (hastily evacuated by an Italian diplomat during the war), the greyish-black asphalt sticking to my shoes, I was confronted by one of them. This one, a short man dressed in World War II military khakis, with a crew cut and a pronounced New Jersey accent, started the conversation by telling me how happy he was to meet an American. How he had lived in America and how he loved America.

He punctuated each statement with gestures. After a couple of minutes of this, he got to the point: he had heard, he said, that the newly arrived Americans were in need of toilet paper. Strange he should be so well informed.

During the war, the Egyptian government suspended sales of paper products, most notably toilet paper, on the grounds that paper was needed for military purposes. The only toilet paper to be found was in the bathrooms of the major hotels or the university. Not a good situation for newly arrived Americans. The choices seemed simple and unpleasant: soak the ink 'off' daily newspapers (my favourite was the *Egyptian Gazette; al-Ahram* was too bulky), use rags or learn to navigate traditional facilities. Each had drawbacks: the ink never really came off, the rags were unpleasant, and Egyptian detergent didn't really help.

The traditional facilities, the lineal descendants of Roman design, consisted of a hole in the floor, sometimes with a short standpipe and hose; and while elegantly simple, they smelled of urine and worse. Worse than American outhouses? Certainly not. But the traditional facilities were unacceptable to Americans fresh 'off' the boat, all the same.

For the men, this was a nuisance, but for the women, it was a real hardship. They were forced to either steal from the university bathrooms all the toilet paper they could carry in their purses, or rent rooms at the Hilton and do the same, at some expense.

So, after another short parlay, we arrived at a price for 200 rolls and agreed to meet the next day. I told Broome about the arrangement during a break between classes. His eyes lit up with the promise of riches. "We can corner the market," he exclaimed. Never mind the black-market implications; it was the right thing to do, especially given the exigencies of the situation. The next day, I handed over the money, and within an hour, two men delivered a very large carton to the apartment. Now, what to do? I immediately told the ladies and arranged for both access to the apartment bathroom and a toilet paper roll. They seemed grateful.

Unfortunately, this happy state of affairs lasted exactly two days. On the morning of the third, I was forced to attend a class in Islamic historiography delivered in classical Arabic by Dr Sakut. A renowned historian, Dr Sakut was a thin, wiry man who made no concessions to American students and in fact seemed to regard us with ill-concealed contempt. He conducted all of his lectures in classic Arabic. In practical terms, this meant that I understood only about half (on a good day) of what was said.

As I sat there, miserable anyway, I looked around and saw nothing but frowns and glares. The class droned on, and I felt an increasing sense of unease. Something bad was going to happen. I thought to myself that this foreboding must have been what Harry's men experienced as they watched the French knights slowly assemble at Agincourt in preparation for a massive charge ("Harry, that looks like really big trouble."). Perhaps, I should have brought my chain-mail shirt.

When the class ended, I figured on making a quick run to the safety of the student lounge for a cup of Turkish coffee. Miserable but safe. Too late. The hallway was blocked by a phalanx of angry ladies. So, like Andre Chenier (to change the metaphor), I strode forward to meet my fate. Tia, like a blonde Queen of the Night, swooped to meet me.

In tones a mother might use to discipline a rambunctious child, she said: "We've had enough of you and your nonsense. For months now, we've watched you slither through classes without doing anything. Look what you did to Professor Khoury; you knew that he was deaf in his left ear and blind in his left eye. You deliberately sat as far to his left as you could, knowing he couldn't hear or see you. Then you would run up after class and compliment him on his poetry and coo over pre-Islamic qasidas. You got an 'A' without ever opening your mouth."

"Worse, Mr Vulnerable, you sweet-talked us into doing most of your homework. Rosemary almost had a heart attack because she did all your extra work. Now we're not going to put up with you and your toilet-paper shenanigans. You act as though you are a junior-grade Suleiman the Magnificent and your bathroom is the Sublime Porte. You insult us as women and you betray us as Americans."

To no avail, I mumbled, "I wouldn't go that far." But, clearly, Andre was going to have a bad morning.

Furious now, Tia threatened, "You split it up, or else you get no more help from us. Don't kid yourself. These Egyptians don't give a damn who you are; they'll flunk you out as soon as they look at you. And then it's off to the U.S. in disgrace."

Sun Tzu, or it might have been Wellington, once observed that a wise general knows when to retreat. Tia's final threat was too real. I conceded at once. The scowls turned to smiles. "That's better," Tia relented. "Rosemary has a phone, like you. You can call her for help anytime. The rest of us will pitch in. The language lab is your problem; we can't help you there. Maybe you can sweet-talk the Egyptian staff. We'll be by at three." And they were.

Anyway, the Egyptian government soon solved my original problem by resupplying toilet paper. So much for venture capitalism. And, I was happy to still be alive. However, the language lab required some thought: as Holmes would say, "It was a two-pipe problem."

At lunch, I often enjoyed a bowl of 'mulukhiyah' (a spinach-like soup). Nobody else in the group would eat mulukhiyah; they would all make faces and say, "How can you eat that stuff? It's like slippery spinach." "It's no slimier than boiled okra." I would generally reply, "And since you're in Egypt, you should at least try a national dish." But this impeccable logic usually fell on deaf ears.

During one lunch, Rosemary came over, sat down and watched me. "You know, you've been eating so much of that terrible stuff, you're turning green." Then, looking more closely, she observed, "Aha, I see that you're growing a beard. Is that deliberate, or are you just sloppy? Now that I think of it, you are beginning to look like an imam and a green imam at that." Then, she laughed. "That's it! Now all you need is a long, a very, very long, green beard to complete the picture." And she stroked an imaginary floor-length beard. In Sunni Islam, imams are the leaders in prayers – an important societal role – but they are often treated colloquially as figures of fun. But Rosemary was not done. "You'll be the first green imam in Islamic history. People will come from miles around to visit your green shrine." And except for the green part, she wasn't far off. I shaved the next morning.

About two months after the toilet-paper revolt, when I was about halfway through a bowl of mulukhiyah, Broome appeared, his brown moustache on alert. Breathlessly, he announced, "I've made a discovery. The American Embassy has thousands of Egyptian pounds. I've been in the embassy basement, and there are carts full of pounds. They can't get rid of them, and they're willing to give them to us for fifty cents on the pound." (The official rate was three dollars to a pound.) "All we have to do," he continued, "is exchange our student support checks (in U.S. dollars) for Egyptian pounds at the embassy, instead of using Egyptian banks."

I said, "Broome, have you considered what the Egyptian government might think of this arrangement? Does the term 'money laundering' come to your mind?"

Without hesitation, he replied, "Look, there's only eight of us, and the U.S. checks are very small; nobody will notice and it's marginal anyway. Besides, we can live like pashas."

We all talked about this at some length. But since this sounded too good to miss, we adopted Boss Plunkitt's maxim: "I seen my opportunities and I took 'em." And it did seem like honest graft because we were not actually stealing money but rather were helping the embassy get rid of unwanted Egyptian pounds. It was a noble enterprise. The arrangement worked like a charm for a month or so; we walked over to the embassy (technically closed because Egyptian-American relations were broken off during the war) and exchanged the checks. Nothing happened; nobody seemed to notice.

But of course, somebody did notice. That discovery was inevitable should have been obvious, because the embassy clearly was under surveillance. At any time, there were two or three men in brown suits leaning against the grey embassy walls reading *al-Ahram* (once, I saw one of them 'reading' an English-language newspaper upside down). But then, the whole of Egypt was bugged. When we first entered the Garden City House, I saw an open doorway off to one side of the dark mahogany marble staircase at the end of the lobby. The room inside had a long, brown table and a line of sitting Egyptians wearing large earphones. I waved. They looked up, smiled, waved back and then continued listening.

Whenever Rosemary and I talked on the phone, we could hear heavy breathing from someone listening. Sometimes, just for the hell of it, we would invent crises and breathlessly describe imaginary mobs heading toward the city's centre. For months, I was regularly followed by a white Fiat (every other Fiat in the city was blue). I debated as to whether to ask the occupants for a ride, since we were all going to the university. But caution always got the better of me.

While the near constant surveillance was worrisome, we eventually became used to it. It was a curious experience to live in a country where your every move was watched. I think that I began to understand, dimly, what the Germans and Russians experienced.

Egypt was an authoritarian regime, and everyone was watched, particularly those identified as coming from other parts of the Middle East. My mail was regularly opened – and carefully taped back together with official-looking yellow tape. Whenever I received a neatly taped envelope, I would wonder whether it might be followed by a pounding on the door.

But there was more. The apartment where the Broomes and I lived had an office of the American Friends of the Middle East two floors below. "Who are these Friends of the Middle East?" Broome would ask with a sinister smile.

"My guess is they're CIA," I would reply nonplussed. And, indeed, years later, a newspaper reported that the 'Friends' were a CIA front. Occasionally, Broome and I would have to trundle up five flights of stairs to our apartment when the power went out and the ornate Victorian elevator stopped working. Power outages were common in Cairo, but to my delight, every time the power was restored, the whole city would break out in cheers and applause; the Egyptian sense of humour knew no bounds. Anyway, our trundling regularly brought us past the 'Friends' door. On one occasion, Broome gave it a push. It creaked open. We looked at each other momentarily and then went in.

The several rooms were nicely furnished: Egyptian baroque green-leather furniture (green, the Prophet's colour, was a nice Islamic touch), Egyptian carpets and several 'pouts' (ottomans) on the floor. All this, plus shelves of glossy printed materials. But what really caught my eye was a large aquarium with tropical fish. Now where did they get that? I peered in and then said, "Look at this." Immediately, lights in the Mugamma (central administration building) across the street flashed on. "Broome, come here," I called out to him. "I just spoke into the fish tank and the lights went on. Now that's a creative place to put a bug. I think it was planted on the Jack Dempsey; that's a very suspicious-looking fish." Broome was not amused.

"I think we should leave," was his only comment. So, we quickly and quietly left, carefully closing the door behind us.

The surveillance went even further. After a couple of weeks, the Broomes and I decided to hire a cook to do the shopping, cooking and general housekeeping. I asked around at the university and, soon enough, a candidate appeared. His name was Aswad. He was a Nubian and did not speak a word of English or Arabic, which meant that we couldn't communicate with him outside of sign language. No matter, he proved to be quite good at his job; our food costs went down, the place was cleaner and the meals definitely better. That is, until one day.

Early one Sunday morning, there was a huge boom and all the windows rattled. Air raid sirens all over Cairo went off. The ruckus was deafening. This was usually caused by Israeli Mirages streaking over the city: an insulting demonstration of Israeli military dominance. Sometimes the jets actually made bombing runs; according to the Egyptian press, on one such run they had bombed an elementary school, killing several children. After the first sonic boom, I asked a shopkeeper (I was buying coffee at the time) what was happening. He replied, "It's the Israelis; they want to see the pyramids."

I went to the dining room window overlooking Tahrir Square and looked out: traffic was moving as usual; people were walking; the 'bawabs' (apartment managers) were sitting and laughing. Nobody seemed to care. *Wonderful*, I thought, *they're giving an air raid, and nobody's coming.*

But surprise, surprise, Aswad ran out of the kitchen and yelled in perfect English, "Air raid, air raid!" After a sheepish moment or two, he signed that he needed to go shopping and left. He didn't return.

Even so, I and everyone else in the group became used to the constant surveillance, even to the point of discounting its implied threat. In what should have been an obvious warning, I had met Kamel Husayn sometime before. Husayn was in Nasser's cabinet, ostensibly as minister of 'Social Affairs', and was widely thought to be Nasser's chief enforcer. He was known locally as 'the butcher of Cairo'. He had been the chief judge in the show trial of Muslim Brethren militants, including their leader, Sayyid Qutb, who were convicted and promptly hanged (from then on, there was a state of permanent war between the Brethren and the government). He was also said to be responsible for the disappearance of hundreds if not thousands of people, of anyone even suspected of political opposition. We had heard stories of desert concentration camps where prisoners sent by him were tortured and then eaten alive by wild dogs.

At one point, he was put in charge of Egyptian school curriculums, succeeding the (blind) dean of Egyptian literature, Ta Ha Husayn (no relation). The letters 'Ta Ha' ('mysterious letters') introduce 'Surah' (chapter) 20 in the Quran. Kamel Husayn brutally changed his predecessor's emphasis on broad, general education and literacy to an enforced school-wide program of political indoctrination.

Ta Ha Husayn was enormously famous as a writer and a proponent of nationwide literacy. Under his management, the Egyptian literacy rate had doubled. I had read Ta Ha Husayn's trilogy *Stream of Days*, one of his best known works and found it to be an incredibly moving account of Egyptian life. Clearly, Ta Ha Husayn was a literary master. He, along with Naguib Mahfouz, produced a body of literature that matches anything in the West and one that certainly deserves more translation. The change in school administration was not for the better.

In person, Kamel Husayn was smallish and puffy-looking, with unnaturally soft-appearing skin. Unpleasant enough, but it was his eyes that were striking; they were blank, devoid of life or emotion. I looked into them; death looked back. His movements were oddly fluid. He spoke at length. He was charming and courteous to the point of unctuousness. My impression was that he was the perfect and relentless serial killer.

An American professor who was visiting the AUC happened (unwisely) to say something derogatory about Nasser in front of Husayn. At dawn the next morning, he was arrested, briefly interrogated and packed on a plane to the U.S. Later, he couldn't understand why. I asked him, "Did you know who you were talking to?" He said no, that he was just making conversation. I left it at that; I didn't bother telling him that he was probably lucky to be alive. But I thought it. We were fortunate that Husayn did not determine our fate. God may or may not protect fools, but he obviously protected American graduate students.

Came the deluge: Broome for some reason had exchanged a $4,000 cheque, and that was just too much for the government's patience. The uproar was tremendous. Our local advisor, Professor Williams, who always wore a pearl stickpin and spoke in a precise Princeton accent, was summoned to the university president's office. There, he was confronted by enraged senior Egyptian officials who threatened both to throw us out and to close the university. He came out of the meeting clearly shaken and seemed at a loss for what to do. Even his stickpin looked dejected. That brought Brinner to Cairo on the run.

He arrived a day after the initial blow up and herded us into one of the smaller classrooms. Pacing angrily back and forth, he demanded to know what we thought we were doing. "You are acting like imperialist stooges," he thundered. (That was Nasser's favourite epithet.) "You have no sense of responsibility. We send you here at great expense, and you betray us." Dramatically now, he went on: "You deserve to be thrown out. You are all worse than 'kafirs' (unbelievers); you are ingrates; you reject everything we have done for you. You dishonour the whole project. The Egyptians would be right to throw you out or even throw you in jail. I never want to hear or see anything like this again." He worked himself into a fury. I thought that I even saw flecks of foam around his mouth. Then he stomped out. Since I had known him only as a mild-mannered Islamic scholar and unflappable chairman, I was impressed.

But we weren't thrown out. A few days later, a settlement was reached: if we used the regular Egyptian banks, we could exchange dollars for pounds at the same rate the embassy gave us. I thought about that result for a while. Obviously, the Egyptian government had considered the ramifications, and obviously, it had felt that maintaining a relationship with the U.S. was more important than taking action against a few overage graduate students. But there was no denying that we had clearly attempted something that we would never have done in America and had done so without giving a thought to the serious risk involved. Question, then, for us as Americans in a foreign country: what sort of self-entitlement as superior Americans allowed us to assume that we could flout local law with impunity?

However, American self-entitlement was not the only instance of self-dealing, sleaze and exploitation. There was a dark side to Cairo as well, one rarely seen by Westerners. In the afternoons, when I came back from class, I would pass by the 'bawab' and his friend sitting in the building doorway hunched over a backgammon board. They vigorously shook their dice cups, intensely scrutinised the board, laughed and rocked back and forth. Clearly, they were enjoying the game. Once in a while, on a Saturday when I had nothing to do, I would go downstairs and look on and ask them about the game. (After all, Bond played backgammon; why shouldn't I?) They took to teaching me to play.

Backgammon originated in Mesopotamia and spread throughout the Mediterranean world. The ancient Egyptians played a form of it known as 'senet'. Shahs, sultans, Roman and Byzantine emperors played variants of the game: a glittering roster of players. Unfortunately, I was not on that roster. I was a terrible player; the bawabs were far superior, and they grinned and laughed every time they won, which was every time.

Once in a while, they made long faces and pretended to grieve. "Poor, poor 'farangi' (Frank, Crusader), he doesn't know how to play." They pretended to sympathise. *Hopeless*, I thought. *First, in judo I was the only man ever to be thrown on his head a thousand times, and now, I'm going to be the only man ever to lose a thousand consecutive games of backgammon.* (This from a junior-grade Bond.)

Clearly, I needed to improve my skill. I asked Rosemary if she knew anybody that could instruct me. She said, with what I soon discovered was a devious grin, that she could help. We began; the results were the same. Except this time, I was insulted in English. "You men have tunnel vision; you can't grasp the subtleties of the game." And she smiled, coquettishly.

"Wait a minute, the bawabs were men," I objected.

"It's in their genes; they've been playing for thousands of years." She smiled again. "Anyway, you might think of taking up something more in line with your intellectual prowess, say lawn bowling or maybe croquette."

I suavely changed the subject. "You know, these backgammon boards are magnificent, with all that inlay. Do you think they are made in Cairo?" She said that she didn't know. Having successfully escaped the insults, I courteously offered to volunteer. "No problem, I will ask Abdul Masih." A few days later, I did, and he said that they were made in shops behind the Muski. He agreed to take Rosemary and me.

The Muski, otherwise known as Khan al-Khalili, was an exotic bazaar: like the camel train, it was straight out of the *Arabian Nights.* It officially dates from the fourteenth century, but its origins lie as far back as the eleventh century. It is one of the oldest bazaars in the Middle East. It is bordered by two Fatimid palaces, parts of which were converted to commercial use, and it has been the subject of countless Orientalist works, of which the best known (and most imitated) are Edwin Lord Weeks's watercolours.

I always imagined, whenever I went to the Muski, I felt that I had travelled back in time to the eleventh or twelfth century: walking through its overhung, narrow, crooked alleys was like walking through a bazaar in the Fatimid Empire. The place glittered with silks, glassware, rugs, brass, copper, silver (there was a silversmiths' enclave within the larger bazaar). Trays, dallahs, pots and pans were displayed everywhere. Each of the small shops overflowed with merchandise, their owners standing outside, hawking loudly. I went there often and haggled with the shopkeepers.

Once, I bought an antique water glass; it looked authentic, with bubbles and lots of mica, but it was probably fake. The shopkeeper looked at me earnestly and said, "It's Abbasid glass; Shaherazade herself might have drunk out of it." I bought it. Well, who could resist Shaherazade?

The 'Mad Caliph' al-Hakim, who claimed divinity and at one point ordered Cairenes to stay up all night (al-Hakim suffered from insomnia), might have prowled the Muski's original alleys in disguise, looking for miscreants. Al-Hakim regularly patrolled Cairo markets; when he found merchants he thought were cheating, he ordered his guards to sodomise them. Al-Hakim was feared for his irrationality and murderous outbursts; he ordered people killed on a whim. He once forbade Egyptian women to wear shoes, declaring that they should never be seen in public. At age 35, he rode off into the desert and disappeared. Apparently, the ensuing search for him was desultory. Al-Hakim was immortalised in one of Robert Howard's *Conan* novels.

Al-Hakim aside, the Muski was magical, and sometimes it even had surprises. Earlier, toward the end of Ramadan, Nora and I had gone there looking for antiques. As we walked down one of the Muski's streets, someone threw a corncob; it hit me in the back. I expected more, so I turned to Nora and said, "We need to get off the street." Ramadan is the Islamic month of obligatory fasting: for a month, Egyptians get up and eat a small breakfast, known as the 'suhur', before dawn, and then go without food or water until sunset. After sunset, they have a large meal, known as an 'iftar'. These meals usually last well into the night. However, between the very early breakfast and the very late feast, Egyptians get hardly any sleep, and after a few weeks of this, the believers' tempers get quite short. Sometimes these tempers are taken out on foreigners. Hence, for us, the need for caution: probably an isolated incident, but potentially dangerous. We immediately went into the nearest antique store.

The store was quite large. Its walls were crammed with pharaonic relics: ushabtis, pharaonic heads, charred clay pots of all sizes, even large sarcophagi of both wood and stone. Larger granite sarcophagi were littered around the floor, interspersed with glass-topped tables. The whole place was dusty and smelled bad. There were several mummies of different sizes propped up at the ends of aisles.

The owner came over and asked me if I was interested in buying a sarcophagus. "We have a really nice selection." He smiled proudly. "Our collection is better than the one in the Egyptian Museum itself." I looked at the sarcophagi.

"Some of these sarcophagi seem to be newer," I said pointing to the wooden ones.

"Yes," he admitted, "we made those ourselves." Then, correctly guessing that I was an American, he said, "Once you take them to America, you can pass them off as real; nobody will know the difference, and they're a lot cheaper. But if you don't want a sarcophagus, I can show you some mummies. We have the best." He pushed me toward a row of mummies. Disgusting. Nora started laughing at my expression.

"Perhaps something a little smaller," I stalled.

"Look at these." He waved happily toward what looked like a row of misshapen objects. "These are mummy feet."

Mummy Feet! My mind snapped. A doggerel began running through my head:

> Mummy, mummy, mummy,
> The mummy wants a yummy,
> And it sleeps upon its tummy,

> Because its nose is all runny,
> And its arms are icky and gummy,
> But, alas, that's not funny,
> Rather, it's atrociously crummy.

It was catchy, and the meaning clearly came through, but it was not quite up to Robert Frost's standards. Still, if not suitable for an anthology of poetry, perhaps the words could be set to a Cole Porter melody. I could see it in my imagination: there was a glittering ballroom, filled with men (looking like Leslie Howard) in tails and women (looking like Olivia de Havilland) in slinky ball gowns, dancing an elegant foxtrot while Frank Sinatra crooned the words. The orchestra (Glenn Miller, of course) moaned. There was a hint of perfume in the air. Placed around the dance floor were tables, tables covered in white linen and sparkling crystal and each with a tastefully decorated mummy-foot centrepiece. Magnificent.

I returned to reality (sort of). "Maybe, perhaps something even smaller. Do you have any mummy thumbs?" Leslie and Olivia smiled. Nora and I left the store.

At the Muski, Abdul Masih hurried us through the cobblestoned walkways. He turned into a narrow tunnel between the shops with a door at the end. The door opened onto a wide, sandy area, stretching behind the Muski. Gone was the glitter; there were only random piles of old tires and mounds of garbage. There was a slight smell of rotting food. At the far end, a couple of mangy-looking stray dogs nosed and pawed through thrown-out food wrappers. Seeing that I was looking at the dogs, Abdul Masih cautioned, "Stay away from them; they carry rabies."

He led us over to a wall, the back of one of the buildings which fronted in the shopping area. It had a line of small windows with dirty glass and a low, dark wood door. He opened the door and we looked inside. The long room was dark, but I saw rows of tables: children, boys and girls, most between 12 and 13 years old, sat on benches in front of the tables, which were lit by lamps set at intervals. On the tables were small stacks of wooden boxes and bone chips.

I stared at the nearest table. A boy, about 13, dressed in a grimy, grey galabiya sat in front of it. His eyes seemed overly large; his face resembled a photograph of an Area 51 Martian. His bare arms were thin, almost skeletal. He picked up a piece of bone with a long tweezers and stared at the box. Then, with a darting motion like a snake striking, he placed the piece in an inlay pattern on the box in front of him. The strike was a blur. Then he sat motionless looking at the box, unblinking. "Have you seen enough?" Abdul Masih asked. We left.

The final episode happened when I had to make arrangements to leave and get my meagre belongings out of the country. This meant dealing with Egyptian customs officialdom. Western writers have generally written unflattering descriptions of Middle Eastern (usually Ottoman) bureaucracy, and by extension, of the ethics of the whole society. Lane, in an otherwise empathetic description of Egyptian society and culture, spends a whole chapter disapprovingly describing the payoffs, bribery and capriciousness of government officials. Lane is particularly hard on the local 'qadis' (judges) who he says rendered judgments based on bribes and other extraneous considerations. But the qadis' brand of rough justice was probably not that much different from the justice rendered by local justices of the peace on the American frontier. Durrell's account of the Alexandrian bureaucracy is dark with implications of corruption. The term 'Byzantine politics' just about sums up the Western viewpoint about Middle East government and corruption in general.

The problem, of course, is that this is all post-Enlightenment thinking. The Enlightenment represented a change from societies based on personal and communal identities to ones based on contractual and rational relationships. And this, in turn, led to the notion that government officials should not use their offices for personal gain. However, no pre-Enlightenment Western medieval official would have given a second thought about using his position to help himself, a family member or any other communally defined relative. Even in the West, the changeover has been slow and spotty; Durrell described Egyptian bureaucratic sleaze, but he could just as easily have been talking about American political machines of the same era. Boss Crump would have been right at home in Cairo. And, of course, there was always the redoubtable Mayor Daley.

Sociology aside, living in Cairo meant a big-time encounter with the 'baksheesh' system: the Egyptian economy was, in many ways, based on tipping. The average Egyptian made very low wages, basically just surviving, and there were no government benefits such as social security to provide any economic protection. Baksheesh, tipping, was a system that generated supplemental income; it was the oil that made things run.

Some American tourists that I met during my stay were outraged and regarded baksheesh as little more than extortion.

But baksheesh is not outrageous: if you make very little, and you need the money to buy food for your children, it is a necessary income supplement. I had learned to use baksheesh early on: a smile, a small tip and possibly a joke, and things got done. A comfortable and easy system of working relationships and not very expensive: Either you could accept the baksheesh system, and suspend judgment, or you could resist, be uptight, and have a very bad time in Egypt.

But getting my accumulated belongings shipped back to the U.S. was another matter entirely. Since I had purchased Egyptian items, mostly antiques, there might be a problem with both Egyptian and U.S. customs. Moreover, the Egyptians very probably had regulations concerning the export of antiquities. This was not a matter of simple baksheesh; this was an encounter with Byzantium itself. I asked around and was told that it was no problem; all I needed was an 'expeditor'. Now that sounded like hiring the Mafia: would an Al Capone lookalike show up? I made the arrangement.

The next morning, the expeditor appeared, not exactly Al but close. He was an Armenian, dark, of middling height and resembling a smug Peter Falk. "Pile everything you want sent in the middle of the floor," he instructed, "and I'll build a box around it." What a novel idea. He then waxed eloquent, declaiming melodiously, "The box will be made from the cedars of Lebanon, the finest wood. Noah's Ark was built from this wood. It is termite-proof. You can keep it forever." We agreed on a fee. He then proclaimed, "I will personally take it to the airport. You come too. Oh, and you need to bring one hundred pounds in five-pound notes. This is very important." Aha. Now we were getting to it.

A day or so later, two carpenters put the box together. It looked impressively sturdy, and as advertised, it was made of cedar wood that smelled wonderful. I loaded it up, carefully placing well-protected green, leather-bound copies of the Quran and al-Tabari near the top. The expeditor arrived. Two men carried the box downstairs and put it into the back seat of a mauve 1960s Cadillac convertible. The expeditor and I got into the front seat, and he drove this huge vehicle to the airport, scattering traffic and pedestrians, alternating between street and sidewalk all the way. During the drive, I wondered how he could have gotten this elephant into Cairo. Perhaps I had retained a true master of his craft after all.

We slid into a lower-level entrance and into a labyrinth of grimy cement tunnels, and drove slowly past gated rooms, empty cargo vans, and abandoned trucks. The ceilings were low and strung with electric cables; a line of green-rimmed light fixtures with bare bulbs ran along them. The whole place seemed deserted. The dusty silence was heavily, almost physically oppressive, broken occasionally by the muffled rumble of a jet above. Finally, we reached the tunnel's end, blocked by a large rusted iron gate and rolled to a stop. Behind the gate was a long table. Several uniformed men were lounging around. I handed over the cash. The expeditor took it and, like a magician palming cards, made it vanish. He then got out and greeted several of the loungers with an unctuous smile. Everyone shook hands; everyone seemed to know everyone.

Clearly now, I had hired the right man. There was a lot of exaggerated handshaking and smiles. Cigarettes were offered and accepted. More gesturing and handshaking. I sensed, rather than saw, my pounds disappearing. All of this went on for several minutes.

Then two of the loungers picked up the box and carried it through the now open gates. The expeditor approached the long table. On it was a large open book, some sort of log. Two more loungers were standing in front of the table. The box was pried open. The loungers looked in and felt around; they seemed surprised to see the green books. The box was then very carefully reclosed. There was a moment of silence. Suddenly, they moved abruptly aside and dramatically turned their backs. The expeditor rushed forward and, looking at me with a fiendish grin, signed the book with a triumphal flourish.

A few weeks after I got back, the box arrived, unopened, with customs clearances pasted on its sides and apparently untouched by any customs personnel, either in Egypt or the U.S. I remember thinking, *That is how it's done in the big leagues.* Al would have nodded in appreciation.

IV
What Manner of Men

About 5:30 one morning, while everybody was still suffering from jet lag at the Garden City House, Abdel Masih got us all out of bed 'to see the pyramids'. Yawning, we got into a couple of taxis and drove through the deserted streets. It was still dark. As we headed out of the city and along a line of low bluffs, the sky was becoming lighter. We stopped at the edge of a turnout, got out and walked the few feet to the precipice.

I looked at the flat and empty plain below; looming in the morning haze were perfect pyramidal shapes, their rocky imperfections hidden by the mist. The sheer size and geometrical precision were like nothing I had ever seen. My mind screamed, *ALIEN, ALIEN!* For a moment I thought: Erich von Daniken was right; ancient aliens were here. The surreal outline of the shapes was further accentuated by the contrast with a low building next to one of them. But of course, von Daniken was not right; remnants of ancient sand ramps were easily visible from the air, obvious reminders of human activity.

As Karl Wittfogel once pointed out, pharaonic Egypt was a hydraulic society, in which every activity was organised around irrigation for agricultural production; a society directed from the top by godlike pharaohs whose bureaucracy could control water supplies. And with this control, bureaucrats could direct the activities of everyone in the population. With virtually unlimited manpower and decades of time, Egyptian rulers could build almost anything of stone.

Still, the sense that I was witnessing alien engineering never left me. Moreover, the impersonal linearity of the pyramids didn't match the architectural features of other pharaonic ruins, characterised by curved lines and embellishments that were obviously (and warmly) human. The pyramids were cold and perfect, with machine-like precision and without human decoration. I knew about earlier versions, like the Djoser step pyramid, that were clearly human in design. But that didn't change my original feeling that these massive edifices were not built by men or at least not designed by men who thought as we do.

In this, I wasn't alone. The masons (and also the older alchemist Rosecrucian Order) had long been fixated on things Egyptian and particularly on the pyramids. America's founding fathers, many of whom were masons, worked a pyramid into the design of the U.S. symbols and added the all-seeing eye for good measure. This combination was originally engraved on the Great Seal of the United States and then, in turn, was added to the back of the dollar bill by FDR in 1935.

The Egyptian landscape was dominated by the pyramids. They were visible from almost everywhere in Cairo: great grey peaks above the skyline, the constant reminder to all Cairenes of an awesome past. Egypt's major newspaper, *al-Ahram* (the Pyramids), had pyramids on its masthead. Even though they became familiar sights, and their damaged exteriors made them more 'human', I was always vaguely unsettled by their presence. Early on, we were driven around Giza and went into one of them. For what seemed like at least a decade, we climbed down endless semi-lit, airless stairs, with narrow walls and low unbroken ceilings, with oxygen pumped in.

Finally, we were herded into a small room where the air was heavy with age. Looking up at the heavy stone ceiling, I had an immediate attack of claustrophobia; the walls closed in, the room darkened, my pulse raced, and my breath quickened. I imagined an earthquake sending thousands of tons of stone down on me. I almost fainted. I staggered back against Tia, who was standing behind me. With an audible expression of annoyance, she pushed me through the low entrance and out of the room. I wobbled up the endless stairs. Now I knew how Radames and Aida must have felt locked in their tomb and suffocating. Hard to sing under those conditions. Harder still to stay entombed underground. I couldn't wait to get out into the air.

When I did, I vowed never to enter a pyramid again. Radames be damned.

From my apartment in Zamalek, I had a view of the Great Pyramid from my bathroom. In the mornings, I would sit on the toilet, drink a cup of (hard won) coffee, brashly toast 'old Kufu' (Cheops) and wonder what he might be up to that day. But sometimes a little voice would say, *Watch what you ask for; you might get an answer. Look what happened to the Don. One day 'old Kufu' might just appear, and drag you to hell also.*

Kufu aside, remnants of earlier dynasties were everywhere. Sandstorms regularly uncovered thousands of artefacts: ushabti figures littered the desert floor outside of

Cairo. I also suspected that much of the tiling in older buildings came from marble stripped from the pyramids. And, if you wished, the Egyptian Museum would cast any exhibit (within reason) in plaster for a price. Or you could go into Khan al-Khalili and buy an authentic mummy. Easy to tell its authenticity: ancient mummies smelled like dust; recent ones smelled indescribably bad (in some rural areas, mummification was practised into the 1900s). Old or new, I found mummies repulsive. Still, for the collector of antiquities, Cairo was an open-air museum.

For the average Egyptian, though, these ancient grandeurs were a constant reminder of a lost golden age when Egypt ruled the known world. In a sense, Egyptians (meaning especially Cairenes) suffered from a double whammy. As Arabs, they suffered from the sense of decline from the lost glories of earlier Arab and especially Abbasid, caliphates. Magnificent Islamic edifices dotted the Cairo skyline. As Egyptians, they had the additional humiliation of a sense of decline from an even greater civilisation that had flourished for millennia rather than centuries.

However, a nostalgia over a past golden age is problematic since nobody really knows what that age was like. As Woody Allen (of all people) pointed out: everyone has a golden age that they long for, but that golden age is not real; it is an illusion. The real golden age is the present. Nevertheless, that illusion has present-day consequences.

Much of Arab (and specifically Egyptian) political behaviour that seems irrational to Westerners stems from a subliminal desire to regain this lost (or purloined by the West) greatness, this lost honour. In a curious perceptual inversion, at least part of the Arabs' self-image is due to Western image making. Edward Said argues that Orientalism taken as a whole is a cynical Western mind-set that underlies and legitimates Western power projection; it contrasts the 'dynamic' Western culture with the 'static' or even 'decaying' Middle East culture. But Said understates the influence of the Romantic Movement that swept Europe from the late eighteenth and nineteenth centuries: Romanticism depicted everything in an exaggerated, over-emotional manner, and that depiction included Middle East subjects as well. The influence of the Romantic Movement was far broader than any imperial impulse. Said's argument has been criticised by Bernard Lewis (himself a former British intelligence officer) as being simply anti-Western.

Probably a simpler explanation is that Orientalism is one, out of many, instances of the explosion of cultural energy unleashed by the Industrial Revolution, an energy that brought with it a feeling that the world was for the taking. Hence, the tremendous urge to explore the hitherto unknown and the vicious debates at the London Geographical Society (which started out as a dining club). There was also a sense of wonderment at these new geographical and cultural discoveries that went beyond the political impulse to dominate.

Both Said and Lewis are right in their interpretations, even though each has flaws. A major problem for historians and social scientists is that of where to take a stance: the observer can be detached, outside the academic subject, or can become a participant, inside the subject. Each has its strengths and limitations. The outside observer can analyse behaviour with impersonal and critical detachment: A. R. Radcliffe-Brown and Talcott Parsons analysed societies at arm's length, but at the cost of missing the emotive component, the subjective meaning to their members. By contrast, the participant observer can capture emotional meaning but at the cost of becoming an advocate and losing all sense of perspective. Anthropologists, in particular, have attempted to overcome this dilemma by embedding themselves with their subjects and then theorising. Bronislaw Malinowsky did this in his study of Trobriand islanders. But embedding is not the same as growing up in a culture.

When Said expresses disdain for Westerners who do not understand Islamic culture and bring their own cultural biases to boot, he becomes an advocate. When Lewis rejects Said's anti-Western bias, he ignores his own belief in Western superiority and even (oddly enough) his own dislike for his subject matter.

Be that as it may, Western imagery of Middle Eastern subjects has been around since the sixteenth century, in art and in music as well: think of Mozart's *Abduction from the Seraglio*. But Napoleon's 1798 invasion of Egypt provided the real impetus: the French dispatched a team of artists and scholars who created a cache of superb 'Orientalist' works. Augmented British interest in Middle Eastern oriental subjects probably dates from Nelson's victory in the Battle of the Nile, also in 1798.

From there, following Western political expansion, Western artists produced magnificent works. Some were based on actual observation (usually watercolours of camels, pyramids, markets and palm trees), but the majority (the bigger oil paintings of harims, slave markets and snake charmers) were pure fantasy. Many of these works were rooted in a prurient interest in the harim system: a system of political alliances cemented by the exchange of daughters, similar to Western feudal alliances but more organised and extensive.

However, the mere fact that no Westerner would ever have been allowed to enter a harim didn't stop Western artists from depicting semi-nude women in various exotic 'harim' settings.

Contrary to Western images of turbaned men sitting around amid acres of ornamented tiles, ogling undulating 'odalisques' (court ladies), harims were all business, their politics merciless and played for keeps. The Ottoman harim at one point had over 3,000 women, plus their children and retainers. They lived in some 400 apartments. Births were carefully recorded because of their implications for succession. Male heirs were housed in mini palaces known as 'kafes' (cages) under permanent house arrest to prevent them from attempting to assassinate their fathers. Some heirs were systematically executed. There was also an attached farm system for generations of bureaucrats: both men (pages) and women (the women in the harim itself) were trained in administration. Graduates were later married. The whole was overseen by the sultan's chief consort and a regiment of eunuchs: a very complex bureaucratic operation with defined roles and positions symbolically identified by florid titles and distinctive headgear. The regime's chief executioner, for example, was known as the 'bulbul' (nightingale) pasha: a poetically fitting name.

When Kemal Ataturk decided to impose a complete cultural break with the Ottoman regime, he announced a simple policy: all heads caught wearing Ottoman headgear would be chopped off immediately. It worked. But the

Ottoman regime itself had already lasted almost a thousand years.

The Western imagery even extended to miniatures of Arabs dressed exotically, praying, selling rugs and women or riding camels. Known as Vienna bronzes, these figurines captured the fancy of otherwise staid Viennese burghers in the late 1800s. Franz Bergman, the most famous bronze maker, cognizant of Austrian middle-class prudery, was careful to sign his more erotic pieces (such as a small sarcophagus that opened to disclose a nude woman) 'Nam Greb', Bergman spelled backward.

The Austrians (and especially the Viennese) had good reason to be preoccupied with Turkish/Arab matters; the Ottomans had laid siege to Vienna in 1683 and were only driven off after a massive cavalry charge (the largest in history, with some 20,000 Polish and Austrian horsemen). Still, the figurines showed Arabs in curiously quaint eighteenth-century costumes (pay no attention to the outrageous Western dress of the time), and at least the Arabs did not wear wigs.

Mamluk palaces in Cairo were less ornate, smaller and certainly less well organised than their Ottoman counterparts. At one point, we were taken on a tour of the Beshtak palace. Impressively large, brownish and adorned with Mamluk architectural elements, it was originally seven storeys tall, now only the lower floors remain. The palace was built over the ruins of an earlier Fatimid palace, and all floors were engineered to have running water. Although now silent, as the administrative centre of the sultanate it must have been occupied by hundreds of officials. The now barren halls would have hummed with conversation and the noise of people moving about.

On the second or third floor, our docent led us down a narrow corridor. At its end was a large (at least seven feet tall) 'Ali Baba' jar. The docent pushed a spring and the jar slid aside. A low archway appeared. We entered a dark, narrow gallery with a wooden floor and decayed remains of benches on one side and high arched windows covered with 'mashrabiya' (latticework) screens on the other.

The gallery smelled old; the floor was unsteady; dust was everywhere. I looked out two storeys below, there was a courtyard slightly smaller than a basketball court, its floor covered with ornate brown and green tile and stylised Arabic inscriptions – not as opulent as Topkapi (the Ottoman palace in Istanbul) but still magnificent. The docent said that the courtyard was for visitors, and the gallery was designed to allow concealed observation of them. But I suspected something different: mashrabiya, when used inside, is usually reserved for harims (hence the term, 'harim window'). Sultans would sit behind the screen, watch odalisques dancing below and choose one for the night.

Presumably, the sultan would walk up the corridor to the jar and its hidden gallery, leaving the clatter of the palace behind. He would enter and stride past the benches, now covered with ornately decorated, tasselled cushions and stand at the mashrabiya window, hands resting on the wooden sill. Below, the orchestra would file in, take their seats, cross-legged and tune up. Maybe they would play a song or two. Then, waved on, the dancers would stream across the floor, billowing colour, perfectly made up, with jewellery flashing.

As for the odalisques themselves, for many, this was a major event, not unlike winning a beauty pageant. Except that here the stakes were much higher: the chosen one could produce an heir to the sultanate itself. Probably they looked up at the lattice-covered window and wondered if the sultan was really there watching. Was there a hint of movement, a sense of a presence behind the darkened mashrabiya? And they were all probably nervous: smile and stay on the beat. All of them would be dancing to traditional orchestration: the 'tawla' (drum), the 'oud' (guitar), the 'kanoon' (zither) and the 'kamanga' (viol). All of them were most likely trained dancers and adept at handling changes in the music's rhythm. The result was a performance much more artistic and sophisticated than usually depicted in the West: nothing so gauche as Salome's Dance of the Seven Veils and clearly a performance that was very tame compared to the bumps and grinds of American pole dancing.

Standing in the gallery and looking at the beautifully inlaid floor below, I mused on what kind of men would have stood and watched. Were they simply animalistic and bent on demonstrating their power over women, choosing women and – forcing them to submit, in an Islamic version of the Hollywood casting couch? Or were their actions more calculated? Perhaps their thinking went something like this: 'Now who am I supposed to pick for tonight? They're all daughters of powerful tribal families. All of them are good-looking, but they're all a lot younger than I am. Their energy is incredible. Which one was it that my vizier said was key to the next alliance? No matter, I've got to be good; for sure, whomever I choose is going to report back to her father. So, watch the pillow talk. Anyway, these long hours are killing me.' Too jaded? Perhaps. But probably a little of both: the images of the casting couch and of the jaded Sultan describe a multifaceted reality.

The ladies must have taken the floor with the same mixture of anxious excitement that contemporary ballroom competitors experience. The performance could be long or short, depending on the Sultan's whim. The chosen one would leave in a flutter. For some, this would clearly be a relief. But what about the rest? Back to the humdrum of the harim, with maybe another shot in a couple of weeks or months, depending on the number of wives. For the losers who might have had imperial ambitions, perhaps their thinking was this: 'What did I do wrong? I'm better-looking than most of them. I wasn't off time. Father is going to be really disappointed about this.'

The imagery did not last long; my phantasy was interrupted by Tia, who had come up from behind and was standing next to me. "So, Mr Mamluk Sultan," she archly inquired, "are you imagining yourself picking out a dancing girl?"

I turned and (some devil made me do it) courteously replied, "If I was, you would be the most beautiful." Abruptly realising my peril, I sidled cautiously backward, out of range of a possible straight right. The walls quivered. Then the full impact of my faux pas sunk in. I had just antagonised Brunhilda herself; I heard Wagner horns in the background. "Siegfried, where are you when I need you?" But no. She gave me a very long and hard look: a look lasting roughly half a century. Time trembled. My legs turned to jello. Then she turned, muttered something and walked to the door of the gallery. Saved by the bell.

In addition to the general Orientalist works, a specifically Egyptian version of Orientalism developed in the West. It originally appeared in the 1870s, during the American Civil War, but it was given more impetus by Carter's opening of King Tut's tomb in 1922. Egyptian Revival, as it became known, blended Egyptian motifs with Western designs. The Egyptian Revival style permeated the plastic arts, architecture and even women's fashion (Claudette Colbert's costumes in the film *Cleopatra* generated a fashion craze). Egyptian Revival forms and motifs were incorporated into early Art Deco.

This blend of the pharaonic and the Western was unbelievably beautiful in all of its forms: post-civil war silver pieces were magnificently crafted by old-line American silver-makers like Gorham. Egyptian motifs were incorporated into architectural styles and used to decorate glassware and china. Depictions of Egyptian-style subjects dominated early alabaster lamps. Furniture was decorated with Egyptian motifs. The artistic output was breath taking.

Orientalism aside, contemporary Cairo was also saturated with pharaonic symbolism and even pharaonic advertising. Blue Eyes of Horus (good luck) were drawn on many walls; ankhs (long life) were equally abundant. Nefertiti's image (apparently adopted from the famous bust in the Berlin museum) was everywhere but especially on groceries; Nefertiti milk (a brand name which I always thought was slightly porno) could be bought in cartons; Nefertiti wine (not up to French standards) was available in quarts, and there were a variety of other Nefertiti dairy and bread products. Clearly, she must have been a remarkable woman.

Because there was so much archaeological material (some finds layered in single sites, others scattered seemingly at random), making sense of it all was difficult, dating and categorisation were problematical. Archaeologists can distinguish the artistic styles of different pharaonic dynasties (I never could), but all seem to have a common characteristic in that Egyptian public art served a functional purpose. The various dynasties had their own idiosyncratic styles; most representations were highly stylised and crafted to present specific images. Ancient Egyptian artists could produce photographic realism but chose not to. Just like Picasso, they could obviously draw, but like Picasso and the Cubists, they were concerned with representing a different, non-photographic reality.

The conundrum for archaeologists and historians was to place these styles, and their underlying societies, into some chronological order. Flinders Petrie, one of the more colourful Victorian characters and the founder of modern archaeological methodology, developed sequence dating: the cataloguing of artefacts according to successive levels in a site, rather than haphazard digging that produced jumbles of finds. This allowed archaeologists to produce chronologies and get a sense of historical development.

Flinders himself was a ferocious figure on the dig; a large man dressed in robes, with a Moses-like beard and flowing hair, he would exhort his diggers by firing off shots from an overly large pistol. Not satisfied with his brilliant but mundane body of work, he developed a theory of the cycle of civilisations. The rise and fall of civilisations, Flinders posited, could be observed by looking at the lead and lag of a civilisation's representational art. In developing civilisations, art evolved, becoming more complex and detailed; in declining ones, the reverse occurred, and art became gradually more simplistic.

In less than 150 pages, in his book *The Revolutions of Civilization*, Flinders settled any issues anybody might have about civilizational change. True? Probably not. Intellectually satisfying? Indeed so. The book provides an insight into the chutzpah and drive of one of the men who shaped Egyptology. But it also illustrates a way of looking at the Middle East that was characteristic of Victorian and later intellectuals: an imperial statement of reality.

Petrie also had some very strong views about the racial origins of the Egyptians, arguing that they were Hamites (Caucasoids). His equally renowned opponent, Wallis Budge, held the quite different view that they were originally African (Negroids). The two engaged in a titanic battle in learned journals. Petrie had much the better of it; most scholars agreed with his views. But Budge was no slouch: as keeper of the Department of Egyptian and Assyrian Antiquities, he built a collection second to none. Moreover, he was a raconteur of note and a prominent figure in London literary circles (he was a good friend of H. Rider Haggard).

Although the debate between Petrie and Wallis Budge was intellectually arcane and scholarly, their views had major political implications for Victorian imperial policy. Everything the Victorians and their heirs theorised about the Middle East, from notions of the 'white man's burden' or the 'Levantine personality' to the 'Sick man of Europe' was based on some academic view. (think of Darwin's theory of evolution, which was politically transmuted into Social Darwinism). Although originally driven by a Faustian desire to extend 'scientific' methodology to historical or archaeological studies, these scholarly debates defined the paradigm that underlay the exercise of technologically superior Western military power. This was a far cry from the Middle Ages when Islamic civilisation was clearly culturally superior and Christian and Muslim military technologies were at parity.

Toward the end of our year, by now tired and jaded, we were taken on a Nile cruise (on the 'Osiris', of course). We floated up the Nile, past belts of green dotted with palm trees on both banks, seeing the occasional camel and watching 'felukas' (sailboats) moving serenely on the water. It was a scene worthy of an Edwin Lord Weeks watercolour: an idyllic setting, an orientalist vision of a world that existed only on tourist brochures. But like a Watteau painting of milkmaids in pre-revolutionary France, the charming picturesqueness concealed a much grimmer reality.

On both banks, the 'fellaheen' (ploughmen) who eked out a living by farming suffered from chronic malnutrition, parasites, endemic waterborne diseases and lack of medical care. The primary illness was schistosomiasis (bilharzia), a disease spread by snail-borne parasites that lodge in the intestines and cause bleeding and anaemia. Those infected, if left untreated, become progressively weaker and unable to function. The fellaheen were lucky; the North African parasites lodged in the brain and caused insanity and death. The fellaheen's lives may not have been exactly 'nasty, brutish, and short', but they were close enough for practical purposes.

The Nasser government undertook programs to reform agricultural landholding, introduce literacy and medical services and control Nile flooding cycles (for example, by means of the Aswan Dam) – it was a work in progress. Nasser also seconded his most competent midlevel military officers to the mayoralties of Delta towns to create efficient municipal administrations. But the task was herculean: the high Egyptian population growth (paradoxically made higher by increased medical services and the resulting reduction in the infant death rate) outran improvements in social services. It was the Red Queen's race writ large.

Nora and I were natural companions on the trip. Both of us delighted in Egyptian antiquities and would share our pharaonic trophies. Cairo was full of antique stores; one could buy anything, from mummy beads, to a mummy itself (if you must have a mummy), to a multi-ton sarcophagus (the airfreight was a little dicey). I preferred ushabti figures, miniatures of the pharaohs' servants placed in his tombs to serve him in the after world, a practice that apparently dated from the Old Kingdom (about 2700 BC). Nora collected scarabs, symbols of the regeneration of life dating from the First Intermediate Period (about 2100 BC). Both were magnificent art forms, designed to express Egyptian beliefs about the cycle of life but works of art that stand on their own. Whenever a dust storm hit Cairo, the desert would be littered with ushabtis and scarabs.

In the Valley of the Kings, Nora and I were in our element: the valley, across the Nile from Luxor, is really a series of valleys and barren hills, part of a larger area termed the 'Theban Necropolis' that includes a second Valley of the Queens. For over 400 years (1500 to 1100 BC), kings were buried in elaborate tombs cut into the limestone hills. The entrances were concealed to protect them from grave robbers

– it didn't work; most of the tombs were looted (with a couple of famous exceptions). We ran through the long tunnels of rooms. At one point, we entered what appeared to be an empty limestone-walled room. Nora shouted, "Look up. Look up." I did. A dazzling vault of stars in a dark sky opened above me. I wondered, *who was this person entombed here so long ago? Did he go out from his palace at night and look up and ask (like we all do), 'I wonder what's out there?' Or was it something else? Did he desire to leave the door open to walk among the stars at the end?* Ironically, the ancient pharaoh and the modern astronaut would have shared exactly the same dream.

We left the valley and drove to the tomb of Hatshepsut, a formidable woman. The wife of Thutmose II, after his death she ruled as coregent with his son, Thutmose III. In practice, she ran the show for over 20 years. Her building projects are exceeded only by those of Ramses II. She is said to have invented the obelisk. But (and it was a big but) she was operating outside the line of succession; she wasn't the male heir. The knives were clearly out. History doesn't record how many attempted assassinations she survived, but finally, she died. Thutmose III, her junior coregent, moved at once to deface her images. Successor pharaohs continued destroying any trace of her statuary (not all by any means, because she built quite a lot) and appropriated her monuments as their own. They did their best to obliterate her from history. Curiously, no clear record remains of where she was buried: an oddity for so great a pharaoh.

So, we decided to look for her. We ran up the wide stairs of Hatshepsut's temple, known, appropriately, as 'the Sublime of Sublimes'. A white colonnaded structure that stretched endlessly across the horizon, it was originally surrounded by gardens, with several terraces cut into the hillside. The temple is magnificent. It was built a thousand years before the Parthenon, which, though often cited as the West's greatest architectural structure, seems small and cramped in comparison. As we went under the colonnades, I said to Nora, "Do you suppose Hatshepsut is walled up in here? I hear that nobody has ever found her remains. I think that she was murdered and the body hidden." Nora laughed.

"That's nonsense. Hawass says she died from cancer due to carcinogens in her makeup."

I replied, "Right, instead of 'carcinogens', read 'arsenic'. Remember Napoleon? The Borgias didn't have a lock on poisoning; I'm sure the ancient Egyptians knew something about that as well." We wandered around the temple, knocking on walls, hoping to find a body. But no luck, so we went back to the 'Osiris'.

The next day, we toured the Ramseum. It was a huge pillared structure with giant statues of Ramses II set between the pillars. The temple was Ramses' ode to himself. Ramses thought big; he apparently liked to build big as well. Ramses ruled for approximately seventy years, a testimony to his vigour and his immune system. He finally died from sepsis caused by an infected wisdom tooth. In the meantime, he campaigned in Syria and Nubia and built tombs, monuments, temples and palaces on a grand scale.

He also advertised his prowess: whereas cartouches of earlier rulers were shallowly inscribed and thus easily redone, Ramses ordered his stonemasons to deeply engrave his bas-reliefs, making them almost impossible to alter. Moreover, he promoted himself as a fearsome warrior; Stele show Ramses driving his chariot over piles of penises cut from (presumably) dead enemy soldiers, or Ramses happily sodomising defeated opponents. A little rough for Western tastes? Perhaps. But the messages were clear: 'Cross this man and bad things will happen to you.'

The statues and monuments reminded me of the Nasser billboard in Tahrir Square; and indeed, Nasser made extensive use of pharaonic imagery (including specific posters of himself as pharaoh). We came to the great feet popularised by Shelley in his poem (probably his best work) *Ozymandias*, the Greek name for Ramses II. The thrust of the poem is Shelley's commentary on the fleeting nature of greatness:

> I met a traveller from an antique land
> Who said: "Two vast and trunkless legs of stone
> Stand in the desert…Near them, on the sand,
> Half sunk, a shattered visage lies, whose frown,
> And wrinkled lip, and sneer of cold command…"

Magnificent, but wrong. The limestone feet were indeed huge: slightly smaller than modern cars, and the original statue must have been immense. But the visage and the sneer were crafted by design. Ramses, like any other head of state (think of Louis XIV and Versailles) used monuments as media. The goal was always the same: to project an image that would influence the decisions of other heads of state, a very traditional statecraft. Wittfogel and the hydraulic society aside, Ramses II ruled for approximately seventeen U.S. presidential terms; his accomplishments in terms of a forward foreign policy and domestic infrastructure programs outweighed both Roosevelts on steroids, with a couple of extra presidents thrown in for good measure.

In 1974, the French and Egyptian governments arranged for Ramses' mummy to be transferred to the Louvre for treatment of the fungal condition that was destroying it. The king arrived at the Paris airport in 1976. Charles de Gaulle, who clearly had a sense of history, arranged for full military honours such as usually accorded to visiting heads of state. As the plane carrying the old pharaoh rolled to a stop, its door opened and the remains were carried down a red carpet. The band struck up, the flags dipped, and the honour guard smartly presented arms.

For its part, the Egyptian government issued a passport which read:

> FULL NAME: Ramses II
> DATE OF BIRTH: 1303 BC
> PROFESSION: King (Deceased)

A fitting honour.

After a long stare at the feet, Nora turned to me and said, "I can still feel that man's presence. He must have had an enormous ego to span so many centuries." Then she smiled. "Now, let's have a look at the Colossi of Memnon; I hear they've stopped moaning." The Colossi, two giant statues of Amenhotep III (who also had a pretty big ego) stand in a Nile flood plain. Holes in their stone structure made moaning sounds every time the wind blew. The noise went on for millennia. Finally, the neighbours complained and the Egyptian government plugged up the offending holes. Still, I thought, *How wonderful to hear a sound that was heard for over three thousand years, a sound that ancient Egyptians and maybe Amenhotep himself heard.*

At one point in the excursion, Mark and I found ourselves sitting on a dais in front of an audience of local officials, townspeople and university staffers, in shirtsleeves and galabiyas. Why anybody would want to honour a group of scruffy students, I'll never know, but the local Egyptians had generously accorded us an (undeserved) honour. Anyway, there we were, sitting above everybody else, like medieval kings. The function was organised by the university and the local mayor. It was hot and dusty, insects hummed, and the smell of barbequed kufta wafted by. We were served tea. Mark looked at me, his long face drooping, and said, "There's a fly in my tea."

I responded, "Take your teaspoon and discreetly remove it."

Mark responded, despondent, "It's buzzing."

I sternly replied, "Look, you're an American and visible to a lot of people, act accordingly. Remember the lecture by the sergeant in the film *The Drum*, where he tells his troops that they are guests at a feast and are expected to act the part? And that means eating anything, even if it's boiled eyeballs, with aplomb. So, stiff upper lip, drink the tea." No such luck; Mark managed to spill the cup. But I don't think Egyptian-American relations suffered all that much. The ceremonies lasted a couple of hours, with multiple speeches in Arabic (which meant that I didn't understand most of what was said).

The mayor spoke at length. A former army colonel, he was one of many middle-range officers that Nasser appointed as mayors of villages. The colonel had only been mayor for about a year; he looked every inch the professional military officer, complete with spit and polish. Short and muscular, with a no-nonsense manner, the colonel had survived the 1967 war, and unlike most of the officers there, who fled, he had stayed with his men.

McDonald once told me that the Egyptian high command had recognised (correctly) that Israeli aircraft could not attack Egyptian forces as long as they were closely engaged with Israeli units. The steep angles of attack prevented Israeli Mirages from accurately hitting Egyptian armour; most of the initial Egyptian losses were due to tank-to-tank fire. But the high command kept issuing conflicting orders. Eventually, the bulk of the officer corps abandoned the field, the leaderless troops soon followed, and the result was a disorganised retreat into the killing field of the Mitla Pass. Later, Sadat solved the problem by sending his officers across the canal on the first wave and then marooning them on the Israeli side, so that they couldn't retreat.

Now, as mayor, the colonel was especially proud of the way he had improved living conditions. He literally bounced with enthusiasm as he described his accomplishments. And indeed, Luxor was clean, its streets were paved, and it was apparently run with military precision.

Following the end of the ceremony, we were jammed into horse-drawn carriages for a ride around town. Broome, Marianne, Nora, Tia and I were in one, the rest in a second. We sat knee to knee, and at once, Tia shot me a look that I interpreted as 'keep your knees to yourself'. The carriage started with a jerk, the leather creaking in time to the horses' bells. We drove for a while in silence, the horses' hooves beating rhythmically on the cobblestones. By this time, it was evening. The sun had set and the buildings and streets were outlined in black-and-silver pochoirs, a scene of starkly defined silhouettes-shapes that flickered and distorted as we moved, that enveloped us and altered our outlines: a giant shifting, strobing, all-consuming Matisse montage.

The carriage rolled on over the cobblestones. Then, next to me, Nora reached into a large purse and produced a bottle of arak. She opened it and slugged some down. The bottle was passed. Tia, to my amazement, held it up, chugged a good portion and grinned, her eyes roguish. I looked on, astonished, while my thoughts raced: *That woman must have the fastest elbow in Upper Egypt. I've never seen her smile before.* I looked again. *And she really is gorgeous.* I was conscious of her nearness for the rest of the drive.

After a couple of more passes at the bottle by all of us, Marianne started singing in Arabic, softly at first and then louder. Nora joined in. Tia began following the melody. The song spread to the other carriage. The singing tailed off into the still night. Then a bass voice – it might have been Cohen, it might have been Jack – started singing 'ninety-nine bottles of beer on the wall'. One by one, we all joined in. The song grew in volume and intensity as it absorbed the group's pent-up loneliness and sense of lost identity and threw it outward onto the silent village. A prosaic American drinking song bounced off Arab walls: a song of defiance and reaffirmation echoed into the Egyptian emptiness.

Now we screamed at the driver to race the other carriage. He also had a shot at the bottle and slashed the air from side to side with his whip. The carriage jolted forward, throwing us suddenly back. The challenge was met, and both carriages careened down the hilly streets, the horse's hooves sliding on the cobbles. The horses themselves flattened their ears and stretched out their necks. The carriages alternated, swinging close then wide apart. The sound of hoof and wheel ricocheted off buildings. The strobing patterns flashed into a continuous blur. The energy rose to a crescendo.

Finally, the energy drained and the pace slowed to a walk. When we returned to the 'Osiris', we staggered aboard, drunk and smelling like horses. A bunch of Americans singing an American drinking song? So much for the ugly Americans. But remember, the 'ugly American' was the hero of the book, *The Ugly American.* He was the American who identified with the natives and earnestly tried to help them. And we were in Cairo because we wanted to identify as well. But the emotional cost of that enterprise was heavy; the tension between an American identity and Egyptian cultural immersion was sometimes unbearable and could not always be suppressed.

The next morning, in Karnak, I wandered alone, slightly hung over and depressed, down the Avenue of Sphinxes: a double row of ram-headed statues. It paralleled what once was a reflecting pool but was now a sandy path. I entered the temple ruins. A grand entrance indeed. The temple complex was enormous, over one hundred columns. Once inside the hypostyle hall, I was surrounded by these massive pillars. Their bulk pushed at me. They were crowned with arching lotus leaves, which amplified the heaviness. The original concept had been to re-create the primal papyrus swamp from which Amun arose. The hall had a stillness that seemed to absorb all movement, very much like the stillness I had experienced in a giant-sequoia grove in California. The light was dim, blocked by the columns; only slits of the sky were visible. When the temple had been covered with its wooden roof, the light would have been even more obscure, and acoustics must have been phenomenal; the sounds of conversation, praying or chanting would have echoed contrapuntally throughout. This clearly could be the bottom of a giant swamp; the Egyptian architects had achieved their purpose.

Like Clara in the *Nutcracker*, I was miniaturised. For her, everything – Christmas tree, presents, even mice – had grown to gigantic proportions. For her, it was a dream.

But for me, this was real. Looking up from the swamp bottom, I thought to myself in excited wonder, *this is bigger than Cecil B. DeMille; I'm actually in the set for Cleopatra (which didn't survive the British weather). All that European stuff, the Parthenon, the Roman Colosseum, Versailles (well, maybe not Versailles; Louis XIV thought pretty big), is small by comparison.* But that was a superficial reaction, worthy of a tourist. No, the reality was that this forest of columns conveyed exactly the feeling of reverence and awe that its builders intended.

Leaving the papyrus grove, I walked around the several courtyards, then spotted a tunnel. "Aha. A mystery." I entered and walked along a darkening corridor. Perhaps there were a leftover pharaoh or two lurking in the shadows. Then I stopped, stunned. Unexpectedly, a shaft of sunlight unrolled diagonally across a wall in front of me. It lit up two little girls, each about eight or nine, dressed in royal garb. They must have liked playing in the sun, because they were now bathed in sunlight. I knew that ancient Egyptians would design apertures in burial crypts to allow in beams of light, but this was tragically different.

I could imagine that their father, pharaoh and ruler of the Egyptian world, after a hard day of straight-faced listening to nonsensical petitions, patient reasoning with half-crazed generals, and hyper vigilant watching over scheming courtiers, would retreat to his garden. There, he could sit in the sun, smile and listen to the screams and laughter. But then something happened; the girls got sick. He probably called in the best physicians in the kingdom and maybe even brought in an expert from Assyria. He was powerless. They died, most likely from a childhood disease that a contemporary paediatrician could dispatch with a crisply written prescription. Then, he did the only thing he could do; he made sure that his daughters could play in the sun for eternity. Time collapsed with grief. I turned and left that place of anguish. I went back to the ship.

And the 'Osiris' returned to Cairo.

V
Alas, James Bond

After spending a couple of weeks in the Garden City House, Broome, Marianne and I had moved into a very large apartment on a corner opposite the Mugamma, with a view of Tahrir Square and the Egyptian Museum beyond. Every morning on my way to the university across the square, I would walk by the Mugamma. It was technically a civil-administration building, but we were told that it really was the secret police headquarters. A square, plain edifice, it usually seemed empty; I never saw anyone enter or leave. The sewers adjacent to the building always had an unusual odour, an odour of (human?) decay. Sometimes, when I passed by, I thought I heard faint screams, but that could have been due to an overactive imagination. I would always carefully watch the Mugamma's doors expecting an Egyptian version of Baron Scarpia to emerge. Silent and sinister, the Mugamma embodied the below the surface terror of a police state where people disappeared randomly in the dark.

The Broomes and I split the rent. The apartment spanned most of the seventh floor, with balconies overlooking the square complex on one side, and the American Embassy on the other. Curiously, even though the apartment was many storeys above the street, its windows had steel shutters that could be completely closed. It was elegantly furnished in Egyptian baroque-polished parquet floors and gold-and-brown brocade overstuffed chairs and divans with ornate gold arms and legs. My favourite piece of furniture was a long green and brown couch with gold legs ending in what looked like duck's feet. I could lounge on it and watch old Charles Laughton films, with Arabic subtitles, on the TV.

Oil paintings of King Faruk and other notables hung on the walls. These were supplemented by glass cabinets stuffed with china and crystal. The layout had bedrooms with bathrooms at both ends, with living room, dining room and kitchen in between. The previous occupant, an Italian diplomat who left suddenly in June 1967, was said to have had an extensive pornography collection, but this had been tastefully removed. The Broomes lived in one end and I at the other; and as there was plenty of space, we didn't get in each other's way. These were digs fit for a pasha.

Broome was easy enough to get along with. He and I would usually go to class in the mornings, and after class, I wouldn't see him until late in the evening. I never asked what he did with his time. Marianne (or Henrietta, depending) was a different matter. A slim woman, with dark hair and big brown eyes, she normally would have been quite attractive. But there was an angry energy about her that made me nervous; she reminded me (unpleasantly) of a Fair Play for Cuba activist from Berkeley. I sensed that if I ever crossed her, there might be a truly angry outburst. As a Palestinian, she was outspoken about her hatred of Israel and made no bones about her ambition to strap on an explosive vest and blow herself up in a Tel Aviv market.

Moreover, she hated Egyptians. Once, when it rained in Cairo and people everywhere started taking pictures of this rare event, she remarked, "They're going to sell a lot of hair straightener tomorrow." When I asked why, she said, "Because these people have kinky hair. They're not true Arabs, like I am. We true Arabs have straight hair."

As it turned out, I was right. Marianne was nobody to trifle with. One morning, as the three of us were walking to the university (I was dawdling slightly behind in order to be late to class), a crotch-grabber made a pass at Marianne. Bad idea. He missed; Marianne screeched like a steam whistle and then swung her heavy purse like an Olympic hammer thrower. The purse hit the would-be grabber alongside his head and knocked him sprawling. Parenthetically, while we were still in Berkeley, the subject of personal safety had come up; the possibility of personal attack and the historical fact of brutal mob assault were on everyone's mind. When asked, the instructor laughed and said, "Just yell for help and a thousand Egyptians will rush to your rescue."

And lo: a thousand (well, maybe not quite a thousand but enough) Egyptians did rush out. They chased the youth, now in fear for his life, down the street and then consoled Marianne with apologies and Coca-Cola. I reflected: if Kitty Genovese had been in Cairo, things might have ended differently.

Broome and I initially needed Marianne's fluency in Arabic to negotiate simple things like the price of groceries. Marianne was usually uncooperative and only helped (sullenly) after much pleading. Even when she did deign to translate, she complained about the Egyptians' barbaric Cairene accent, in contrast to her more classically pure

Levantine dialect. Needless to say, I usually kept my distance and was cautiously polite.

But then, one morning, it happened. I usually shaved every morning (except Fridays and Sundays, the two alternating weekend days that I never quite got used to). In an excess of caution, I had brought a couple of Gillette razors and a supply of Wilkinson (Sword) injector blades with me. While shaving, a generally miserable experience, I would meditate on the past glory of the Wilkinson Sword blades that I was using. The Wilkinson Company had made sword (mostly cavalry saber) blades for two hundred years. When both cavalry and sabers fell out of military fashion after World War II, Wilkinson switched to garden utensils and razor blades. Nevertheless, Wilkinson advertised their razor blades as having the same steel and sharpness as the sabers used at the Battle of Balaclava in 1854. Cool. So, while scraping away, I would attempt to ease the pain by imagining the sun glinting off the blades of the six hundred as they charged the Russian guns.

Moving on, I had started reflecting on how it would feel to be shaving with a real saber. When you stop to think about it, shaving with a saber is awkward, given its size, weight and dangerous sharpness. Sometimes, I tried to imagine myself as a corseted cavalry officer (British cavalrymen wore corsets in order to present a slim, fashionable silhouette), complete with pencil moustache, cleaning up for the morning's drill. That morning, my meditation had gone further: *what if I cut off an ear with this saber blade? Then, logically, what if Van Gogh had been using a Wilkinson blade? Would I now feel just as Van Gogh did?* I had just begun to explore this fascinating conjecture, when the bathroom door suddenly opened.

Marianne stood there completely naked. My eyes quickly swept down, the brown hair, the glowing eyes, the half-smile, the tan nipples, the dark triangle, the slightly parted legs. Clearly an invitation.

As my eyes were moving, so was my mind. At once it came to me what Bond would do: Either he would carry her off, masterfully, to bed, or he would cover her with a bathrobe, again masterfully and gently suggest another time. But alas, all I could do was grab a towel (I was also bare) and giggle in embarrassment. What a failure! Bond was outraged. Even Van Gogh was horrified. The smile vanished and so did she.

Things rapidly became worse. In the following days, Marianne and I warily circled each other, like boxers in the first round of a fight. Marianne was purse-lipped, her movements staccato. She avoided my glance, always looking straight ahead. Her anger was obvious and increasing. Paralysed with humiliation, I meditated on 'eunuchdom.' Not only had I failed as a man but I was too afraid of Marianne's anger to risk trying to apologise or doing something to defuse the situation.

Two weeks went by in misery. Then, when I came home late one afternoon, the apartment seemed empty. Suddenly, Marianne popped out of the kitchen and ran toward me. She had a short paring knife in her left hand. She swung the knife. The blade thunked into the cover of Hans Wehr, which I had reflexively thrown up. The knife skittered to the floor. Still holding Hans Wehr, I slammed Marianne against the wall and threatened to bash her head in with it. We stood frozen for an eon. The room turned red. I could feel the energy cycling up to a scream in my head, cycling up to an irreparable violence that I couldn't control. She gave a weak push and the cycling stopped. Hugely relieved, I amplified the push and staggered backwards. Free, she ran to the other end of the apartment, making little mewing sounds. I collapsed onto the couch with the golden duck's feet and contemplated a heart attack.

A week later, the Broomes moved out. Broome explained that he had been looking for another apartment for some time and had just found one closer to the university. I had Hans Wehr rebound in black leather (there were local Coptic monks who rebound books). Shaken, but undaunted, I lived alone in the apartment for the next several months, vowing never to have anything to do with an Arab woman. Later, I was told that Marianne had divorced Broome and married a Saudi diplomat.

Instead of walking directly across the square, I had taken to walking along a short tree-lined street and then along Qasr Ayni to the university. It was a pleasant walk; the morning sun shining between the arched leaves and dappling the street past rows of apartments and the burned-out Kennedy Library. The library was set on fire by African students in 1964, and unaccountably, the nearby fire department failed to respond. These morning walks soon became something more; as I walked (slowly, as usual, so as not to be on time), in the cool, still morning, I would pass lines of bawabs, usually older men dressed in grey galabiyas with white skull caps, sitting in doorways on both sides of the street. They were like a modern avenue of sphinxes stretching to the distant end of the street.

The first couple of times that I went by them, there was nothing but watchful silence, only a general rustling. But then, a voice called out, "O' friend, what time is it?" There was an increased scrutiny from the doorways; I could sense many eyes. I flourished my arm and studiously examined the watch dial.

"A quarter to nine, o' friend." Surprised laughter along the street. This exchange went on for a couple of days. Then, curiosity got the better of them; they surrounded me and started asking questions. Why was I here? Clearly, I was a foreigner, an American? What was it like in America? Were American streets actually paved with gold? And so on. These sessions grew longer; the bawabs took to tutoring me in Arabic, instructing me in colloquial insults. Then they even demonstrated their use of the short clubs (akin to the clubs used by Capone's men in Chicago years before) that they carried.

Finally, one of them produced some 'shawarma' (roasted meat) on pita bread. He said that he had told his wife about me, and she thought that I needed nourishment. She was right. From then on, they would bring a variety of foods and always seemed both astonished and pleased because I clearly liked the food and appreciated their generosity. Soon, they brought out photos of their wives and children. When I asked them jokingly how devout Muslims could have such graven images, there was stunned silence, then roars of laughter at such foolishness from the farangi. The Quranic prohibition against graven images, they explained, had nothing to do with photographs. That was for ancient imams with long beards, and they started stroking imaginary beards.

At one point, they presented me with one of the knives they carried: an eight-inch switchblade made in East Germany; it opened with a satisfying click. It proved to be a useful tool. As I discovered, when inserted between a door and jam, it could open any of the older (Ottoman) locks in

Cairo. Aunt Mamie would have been pleased. The morning walk became an excellent way to start the day and remains one of my fondest memories of the city and the people in it.

One morning, I was slowly walking to the university to attend a class in conversational Cairene: not exactly a heavyweight subject. But I paced myself all the same to come in slightly late (but nothing too obvious) so as to limit any possible recitation time. The class had been going on for about a month and was taught by a relatively inexperienced instructor named Samira. She was said to be the trophy wife of the oldest member of the RCC, a man in his late seventies or early eighties. It was an arranged marriage.

Rumour had it that he had previously gotten her a position as an anchor on Egyptian state TV. Since I had a TV, I watched Egyptian programs. Usually, the news anchors were very good-looking women who spoke Arabic with a slight lisp, which was surprisingly sexy. The other programming consisted of movies, including English- language black-and-white films and interminable sitcoms. The sitcoms all seemed to have the same plot: a young woman was to be forced to marry a decrepit effendi, complete with white handlebar moustache and red 'tarbush' (fez). The heroine would immediately start dying of something the Victorians would have called 'the vapours', until she was rescued by a dashing Air Force officer who usually looked like a young Omar Sharif. I never saw Samira on TV; she might have been on before my time in Cairo.

All the same, Samira was beautiful; she had long, dark hair tied up in a loose bun, big brown eyes, a pale complexion, a round face, and she was slimmer than most Egyptian women. She looked to be of the Circassian type of beauty that was so favoured by successive Ottoman, Mamluk and Khedival elites (and the subject of many Orientalist paintings). I watched her with appreciation, and occasionally, I thought I saw a return glance.

I took my seat (we sat around a long boardroom table), still suffering a slight hangover from too much 'arak' (sweat), or 'zabib' (raisins), as it was colloquially known, from the night before. I had taken to prowling about Cairo's darkened streets in the evenings, like Nayland Smith in search of the elusive Fu Manchu. (Sax Rohmer, the *Fu Manchu* series creator, spent time in Cairo as a London newspaper stringer.) The streets were usually empty after eight or nine o'clock and I could simply wander around as though I owned the place. I would look at shuttered windows, softly backlit and wonder what might be going on inside. The city dreamed in silence.

Anyway, I had discovered a liquor store a few blocks away. I was pleasantly surprised that this most Muslim of cities would have such a sinful establishment. But there it was, looking very much like its American counterparts, complete with a buzzing blue neon sign. Its small space was crammed with all kinds of bottles and brands, even some American but far too expensive. There, I discovered arak, colourless until water was added (then it turned white) and anise tasting. It was deceptively smooth but had the kick of American White Lightning. The glasses I poured it in always seemed to leak; I couldn't tell whether this was from the arak or from just poorly made glassware. As a precaution, I kept arak bottles in the refrigerator lest they explode.

Hangover or not, this morning's conversation was to be about breakfast. This was truly deadly, and the room was uncomfortably hot. I had almost dozed off, when Samira called on me, "O' friend, how many eggs do you eat for breakfast?"

What nonsense. Hung over and half-asleep, I replied, 'Hamsin', fifty, instead of 'hamsa', five. Her eyes lit up, she grinned and said, "Fifty eggs, you must be a mighty man." Before I knew it, she was standing next to me, leaning over. Her hair brushed my face.

I could smell her jasmine perfume. "Are you a mighty man?" she almost whispered in my ear. Even through the headache, I knew at once that I was in over my head on this one.

But I said, "Yes, my love." She flashed back to the front of the class. And a few minutes later, we were done; the class was over.

As the students filed out, the men seemed oblivious that anything had happened. The women, however, had picked up on the exchange. Nora and Leslie smiled faintly as they walked by. Rosemary gave me a knowing look when she came out of the class and purred, 'Mr Mighty Man' as she passed me. But Tia stormed out, pinned me against the wall and hissed angrily, "Just what the hell do you think you're doing? You're going to get us all killed." She was right, and I hated her for it.

Chastened, I walked slowly down the hall toward the student lounge, asking myself how I was going to get out of this. Samira was waiting by the fountain with the dragon's head. So now, I thought, am I now going to play Darley to her Justine? After a few words, we moved to the street – hip to hip, our thighs brushing but no other touching – and discussed matters. She said that her husband wouldn't mind as long as we were discreet. She could arrange for an apartment in Bab al-Luq; her car would pick me up. The car, as it turned out, was a black Mercedes 190 with a cracked windshield and red seats: not as elegant as Justine's husband Nessem's grey Rolls with daffodil hubcaps but good enough.

The next day, after class, I went home and took a shower. Rather than being driven, I walked to Bab al-Luq and the apartment. I went slowly, stepping around an older woman in a niqab squatting and defecating on the sidewalk and dodging a young girl who ran past me carrying a basket of ducklings on her head. It was late afternoon, and the usually crowded street was nearly empty. I squinted at the addresses.

Finally, I found the right one and went in. The lobby was dusty and deserted; the air was much cooler than outside. There was no sign of life, only silence. I went up the circular marble stairs at the back, my steps echoing, passed several empty landings and found the door. I paused and thought, *do I really want to do this?* I felt a lead weight in the pit of my stomach. My mind raced. *What am I getting into this time? This is serious business; this woman is the wife of an RCC member who could have me killed. What if I screw up again as I did with Marianne?* And worse, *What if she just laughs at me?* Then my body took over, and like a marionette, I pushed the unlocked door open and went in.

I was not prepared for what I saw. She was lounging on a brown couch; I could sense other furniture in the room, but I could only see her. She was wearing a white galabiya with silver embroidery and white slippers. Her brown hair, normally up, was down and streamed across the galabiya. My senses blanked out: what a creature! I must have jumped in astonishment because she laughed. *Why*, I thought, *would any woman who looked like that pay any attention to someone like me?* She raised her arms and tilted her head, beckoning. I bent down and kissed her; both of us were trembling. Then I undid her robe and ran my fingers down her body. As I did, I wondered how anything could feel so soft and smooth. Then, my fingers took on a life of their own, hungering for more of the feeling. They went down and down and down.

After it was over, Samira folded herself into a cross-legged sitting position on the couch.

Her elbows rested on her knees, her chin resting on her hands. She smiled and said, "Oh, farangi, now that you've had an Egyptian woman: what do you think?" I think that I mumbled something back; I'm not sure. After all, how do you answer a question like that?

I remembered a comment from Mountolive: "Egyptian women are like Egyptian cats, small and brown, with soft tongues." The 'soft' part was right; the rest was colonial nonsense: Leila certainly deserved better.

Samira went on, "Now I suppose every time you see me in class you're going to undress me with your eyes." She was absolutely and delightfully right; the morning class became much more tolerable.

We began to know each other. In many ways, she was like the women I had known in the U.S. But in other ways, she was quite unlike them; her femininity was expressed differently, and it was intoxicating. Each encounter was an exploration. Each lovemaking changed both of us, as though we were melding our psyches. The small apartment – really only one room with a latticed window that looked out on the street, a few pieces of furniture and a sink – became a place of desire and fulfilment. The time we spent there was far too short.

She told me that she was born in Maadi, which was an upscale suburb at Cairo's southern edge. It was built by wealthy Egyptians as a planned community beginning in the 1900s and was originally settled by emigres and embassy officials. Samira's father was a well-to-do merchant; her mother was from a Turkish upper-class family. Samira was sent to school (through the twelfth grade) at the Cairo American College. There she learned English (the classes were taught in English). After graduating, she went across the Nile to Cairo University. After finishing her studies, she went to work as a secretary in one of the ministries. There she met her husband, a much older man who was a member of the Free Officers and later of the RCC. A marriage was arranged. Shortly after, her father died and her mother left for Europe. I did not ask about her marriage.

Often, after we were done, I would watch her putting on her makeup. She would sit in a striped chair in front of a small white dressing table crowded with jars, perfume bottles and combs. At first, she would sit straight up, then begin combing her hair (its light scent I knew well). She would toss her head from side to side, brushing each side with a long black brush. Then she would look again, sometimes pushing aside an imaginary strand, then smooth an eyebrow, then pat a cheek, and then finally put on lipstick. She would carefully outline her lips, then roll them together, leaning closer to the mirror, looking intently. I watched spellbound, my eyes drinking in every motion, hungry for more.

Once, she must have seen my expression in the mirror, because she suddenly turned and, leaning over the back of her chair, laughed and asked, "Now, just what are you staring at?" I didn't hesitate.

"You," I replied.

The apartment was not the only place we met. Often, I would pass by the liquor store, to the corner where the black 190 with the cracked windshield would be waiting. Samira said that its driver was sworn to secrecy. Late one afternoon, the 190 picked me up. Samira was in the back seat. "We're going to Maadi," she said, "I'm going to show you my old home; it's been empty for years." We drove south through Old Cairo and out to Maadi. We arrived at a low two-storey villa and Samira unlocked the front door. The villa was empty and dusty. The downstairs rooms had dark overstuffed furniture, dark curtains, chevron patterned wood floors and brass chandeliers.

"My bedroom is upstairs," she said and led me up the railing-lined stairs. There was a narrow hall, with a Persian-style runner. She went down the hall and opened a double-windowed door at its end. There was a small balcony with a faded carpet.

We walked to its balustrade. There was a partial moon, and the air was warm, and I could hear sounds echoing from the surrounding low houses. "As a girl, my father would let me sleep here, on this rug, on hot nights," she said. She stepped back from the balustrade and onto the faded carpet and started unbuttoning her blouse. Then she turned, looked sidewise at me under lowered lids and said, "Come here."

In the following months, I went regularly to the apartment. Usually, I would go out the back gate toward Bab al-Luq. There was a small cul-de-sac filled with pushcarts. I would usually dawdle at one of them for a few moments before moving on. My favourite was a cart loaded with copper and brassware. It was owned by a tall, athletic-looking man in a striped beige galabiya. I had known him (the group nicknamed him the 'lissan', the thief) and haggled with him for months.

On one occasion, I asked him if he could find me an 'ibrik' (a long-necked ewer), since he didn't have any in his cart. He smiled and said, "I know of a wonderful ibrik. It's in a fine house, owned by an old lady in Heliopolis. I will bring it tomorrow." Now that sounded like I had ordered a burglary; but I said okay anyway. Sure enough, the next day he had a large copper ibrik; it looked genuine enough. I bought it. Who could resist a genuine antique ibrik from a fine house owned by an old lady in Heliopolis?

After these short parlays, I would walk the several blocks. I got to know (or at least, recognise) the street and its people. The street was usually crowded in the early evenings; people walked by wearing everything from shirts and jeans to business suits, from galabiyas to niqabs.

Western commentators have consistently described the niqab (or burqa) as a symbol of the Middle Eastern oppression of women. Leila Ahmed argues that the Western depiction of veiled women as evidence of an inferior and oppressive culture is an extension of the colonialist narrative. Western painters, when they have portrayed veiled women, have usually portrayed women wearing niqabs as being mere clones of each other. Wassily Kandinsky, in an otherwise beautiful series of woodcuts of Arab women, depicted the women as simple, repetitive patterns. Patterns that he used to create the overall composition: the women could just as well have been inanimate objects. Nothing could be further from the truth.

Lila Abu-Lughod says that 'veiling', wearing niqabs, is a complex behaviour pattern that allows a woman to express her identity in a number of ways, and that the niqab actually provides a feeling of safety since, by definition, it symbolises the woman's inviolability. In my own experience, 'veiled' women in Cairo were not harassed. Both writers also point out that niqab-wearing women are not alike but are easily recognisable by their relatives and friends. Originally, I thought that they all looked the same. But later, I could see the differences between these women in black, and in some cases, even make an educated guess as to what they thought of themselves. And, as that very proper Victorian Edward Lane pointed out over a hundred years before, 'veiled' women could be extremely seductive when they so desired.

Occasionally, I would stop on street corners to let trams and buses go by. Once, when a tram came to a screeching stop in front of me, an older woman in a niqab sitting in the haram section (Egyptian trams had open sections in the middle reserved for women only) patted the bench next to her and beckoned. I smiled, saluted and politely refused. The red-and-white buses were another matter. They were usually packed to overflowing, often with men hanging on to their roofs. Nobody in their right mind would ever ride them; they were just too physically dangerous. A few times, as the buses passed, the passengers (men), seeing that I was a Westerner, would make faces out of the windows and gesture. Sometimes, I gestured back.

Once, I asked Samira about Cairo nightlife. As students, our group saw only one aspect of Cairo: the more traditional and Islamic life of the streets. But I guessed from reading the gossip column in the *Gazette* (and looking at pictures of smiling notables) that there was a very active upper-class social life. The Egyptians apparently had lots of 'celebrities'. She said that she went out often, accompanied by her husband or her brother. I asked her whether she knew how to dance. She grinned and said, "Do you mean 'raqs baladi', or Western-style? I can do both. My father spent a year in Argentina, and he taught my brother and me. My mother learned to belly dance as a girl." I asked her where people danced in Cairo. "We dance in night clubs, away from the street," she explained. "There are a lot of night clubs in Cairo, especially in Zamalek but downtown in Bab al-Luq also. Would you like to go? I can get my brother to take me; he's a colonel in the army. Let's do it this Saturday." She tossed her head, got up and belly danced around the small apartment.

That meant I had to get a date. I asked Nora, but she didn't drink. Next was Leslie, but she was mysteriously busy. I thought long and hard about asking Tia, but that was just too uncertain. Finally, I asked (or rather begged) Rosemary to go. She looked at me quizzically. "So you want to go to a nightclub. You want to party and dance. Have I got that right? Now where are you going to get the money for that? Have you been talking to Broome again?" Then with a grin she said, "So why didn't you ask me first?" (My, how news travels here.) She thought a moment. "I don't know if I have anything to wear," she said smiling now (I knew she couldn't resist). "All right, I'll go, but I think you're up to something."

The nightclub (the 'Shaherazade', what else?) was in an older hotel in Zamalek. Over its door were signs in Arabic and English proclaiming: 'Belly Dancing Every Night.' A doorman checked for our reservation at the entrance. We went in; the club was smaller than I expected. After we were seated,

I looked around. There were small tables, covered in white, circling a dance floor and another tier of tables lining the walls. A few enamelled-glass 'mosque lamps' hung from the ceiling; there were some 'Moorish'-looking arches and long dark-red curtains at intervals along the grey walls. Waiters and busboys were everywhere.

Men and women sat at the tables, their elbows on the white tablecloths. The men wore business suits, some obviously from Bond Street; some wore tuxedos. Most were bare-headed, although there were some tarbushes. The women wore gowns that looked like silk; some wore black cocktail dresses. Clearly, Coco Chanel's 'little black dress' had made it to Cairo. The diners could have been in any city. In front was a raised stage with rows of seats, each behind a red-and-white-tasselled bandstand with the name 'Shaherazade Club' in sequined Arabic. The air was smoky; Turkish cigarettes were mixed with perfume. Everyone was talking; I could make out multiple languages. The room was filled with the clink of silverware and glass. The club was a scene out of an old movie. I looked around again, expecting to see Paul Henreid and Ingrid Bergman sitting at a table, looking longingly at each other; and I felt confident that Tommy Dorsey would take the podium at any moment.

Rosemary and I sat at a table near the wall. The bow-tied waiter in a black vest handed us menus in Arabic, French, and English (one side had European dishes; the other had 'traditional' dishes). We ordered, and (real) champagne was served. Then I saw Samira and her brother come in. The brother was a taller and heavier version of the sister; Samira was in black. The two sat down and ordered. Rosemary followed my stare. "I just knew that you were up to something." She sighed. "I thought I was going to be the belle of the ball." Then, she leaned forward, put her hand on my forearm and whispered, "Please be careful."

The orchestra, trombones clucking, struck up: a foxtrot (good but not great; only an American orchestra can play a true foxtrot), and I asked Rosemary to dance. She was surprisingly 'light'; we danced several dances. The floor was crowded with couples. I could see Samira and her brother dancing, but I couldn't tell if she could see me. The dancing ended and an Egyptian singer appeared; she was young and pretty and wearing a dark-red dress. She sang (in their original language) Arabic, French and American songs. I listened, half expecting her to break into *As Time Goes By* but no such luck. Then the belly dancers came on.

There were several of them, one at a time. They were slimmer and taller than I expected. They all wore spangled bras, long skirts, flourishes of red and gold and spiked shoes. Their hair was long and whipped from side to side as they spun. All were hypnotic: all moved with a sinuous grace, coiling and uncoiling, their skirts and scarves rippling to the music. When one of them took the stage, Rosemary nudged me and sotto voce said, "That's Samia Gamal; she's really famous; she's the Egyptian Ginger Rogers." And indeed, even I could tell that she was clearly superior to other dancers.

A belly dance is structured into movements, fast or slow, that allow the dancer to express herself in the different formats. The musical accompaniment is 'layered', from the underlying beat, to the melodic line, to orchestral flourishes; the dancer can pick any layer to follow. Although dancers have a set 'routine', the actual timing and movement changes with the music. Belly dancing is essentially impromptu; no two performances are exactly alike. American jazz is the closest Western parallel. The belly dance is musically and artistically very sophisticated and is definitely not just mechanical 'bumps and grinds'. At the end of the dance, the dancer goes around the room to collect tips.

Finally, one came around to me. Spotting me as an American, she wrapped her gauze scarf around my neck and invited me to dance. Embarrassed, I declined. "Bond, where are you when I need you?" Rosemary burst out laughing. Then the dancer pushed her hip into my ear and left it there until I tipped her (correctly done, the bill folded over the first two fingers and then stuffed into the girdle). Rosemary, through tears of laughter, said, "Well, at least you got one thing right."

Then the orchestra struck up *La Cumparsita*. I was surprised: a tango in staid Cairo? As Roger Ebert once wrote, "The tango is based on suspicion, sex and insincerity. It is not a dance for virgins." The *Argentine Glide*, as it was known, had been banned in several European countries in the 1900s because of its seductive nature and its origins in Buenos Aires brothels. And I would have predicted much the same reaction in this very Islamic city, but here it was, and nobody in the audience seemed to be aghast; I later learned that tango had been danced in Cairo clubs for years and that tango dancing had been portrayed in Egyptian movies. Apparently, the Egyptians knew about Valentino. And who knows, they might even have heard of the great Argentine tango singer Ada Falcon. I looked questioningly at Rosemary, expecting a 'no'. She nodded "yes." Now I was doubly surprised.

Rosemary and I took the floor. Out of the corner of my eye, I saw Samira reach over and pull her brother up and onto the dance floor. We were the only two couples on the small floor; the rest of the room just watched in silence. I gathered Rosemary into the embrace: tango uses an 'embrace', not a formal ballroom 'frame' – the difference in intimacy is significant. I could see Samira and her brother doing the same. Bodies tight together, in unison, we began to walk (caminar): the Spanish more eloquently describes the intense man-woman introspective feeling of the dance. I executed a rock-turn; and there was Samira in front of me. Our eyes met. Then reality changed and my imagination took over.

I could feel Samira's dark head against my chest; her jasmine perfume enveloped me. We did a couple of slow 'ochos' (swivels), and I sensed the swinging movement of her hips in front of me. Then back to the walks. Samira's warm energy pressed the front of me; our thighs brushed rhythmically. Then I led her to a quick 'ocho cortado' (checked swivel). Samira moved back and forth past me like a whip. I followed with some 'sacadas' ('chase' turns), first slow and then fast, our legs seeming to intertwine. Then some rock steps, moving back and forth in a wave of energy. Then a 'barrida' (foot sweep); I brushed her foot gently but with intention. Then more walks and rocks and a quick 'cadena' (right turn) and we swept around the small dance floor.

Finally, the tango was over, and the illusion with it. I escorted Rosemary back to the table. As we sat down, Rosemary stared at me and said, "Sometimes you astonish me." Samira and her brother left. A little later, Rosemary and I did too.

On a dare, Samira and I broke into the Egyptian Museum. I had told her that I had been through the museum several times but had never seen it at night. "I'll bet that it's pretty scary," I said.

"What kind of nerve do you have, o' mighty farangi?" she shot back and laughed. Late in the evening, the Black 190 drove us to Tahrir Square. We got out in front of the museum. The Egyptian Museum was built in 1902. Its magnificent facade combines Greek revival elements and pharaonic motifs. Its Egyptian artefact collection rivals that of any other museum in the world. We walked past the ornate bronze front entrance and around to the back. There was a set of cracked stone steps leading down to a small door. The door was locked. Opening it was easy; my bawab knife made short work of the lock. We went in, past workshops filled with tables, workshops that looked like chemistry labs, workshops littered with stacks of artefacts.

We climbed a narrow flight of iron stairs to another small door that opened onto the main floor. Hand in hand, we walked past the reception desk and into the main gallery, which was two storeys high with a sky lighted roof. It was lined with statues of bygone pharaohs, set on pedestals designed to replicate their original placement in temples. The line of gigantic statues stretched into the darkness. The silence was heavy; there were no custodians around. We were alone. A few dim lights on stands provided narrow tunnels of illumination; the rest was shadowed. Nothing moved; there was only a feeling of echoing space. As we walked, our steps sounded loud on the tile floor. The cold air around us seemed pregnant with expectancy. Samira shivered and moved closer.

Occasionally, I thought I heard a faint chirping sound from the upper galleries. We continued walking; it was as though we were moving backward into an ancient and unknowable past. We looked at each other and, as if by agreement, stopped.

The floor was hard on my back; my knees were drawn up. I thought we were the only ones moving, but I could feel motion behind Samira, sitting above me. I sensed, rather than saw, the pharaohs on both sides of me stretching up, their faces elongating, craning their necks to see, their eyes widening, smiling. Behind them, their outlined shadows grew longer and arched over us like dark wings. The movement swelled. We finished, got up and went back down the iron stairs and past the rows of open doors and the rooms filled with relics. But the atmosphere now felt subtly different: a sense that I couldn't place, of some vast ancient amusement. Again, it might have been my imagination. We went back up the stone steps and the feeling receded. The night air was warm. The museum door clicked shut behind us.

At one point, a month or so later, Leslie and Rosemary decided that I should go to an Umm Kalsum concert, to improve my 'cultural awareness', as they put it. I objected, saying that I was really a Fayruz fan and that Umm Kalsum was too traditional. It didn't work; I was going anyway. Umm Kalsum was Egypt's most famous singer; her name was a household word. One of her songs became, for a while, the Egyptian National Anthem. Now at the end of her career, she was giving a final concert. The ladies grabbed me by the arms and propelled me into a taxi. When we got to the Balloon Theater, they did it in reverse, dragging me through the glass doors.

The foyer was overflowing and the auditorium was packed. There were no empty seats; people were standing along the back walls. Umm Kalsum came on stage. She wore dark glasses because her eyes had been damaged by years of looking into stage lights. The audience stood. She sang, in a dark contralto, with enormous range. The audience screamed with delight and appreciation.

At intermission, we went back to the foyer. It was jammed, but then the crowd moved away from the centre of the tiled floor. I could see Samira standing at the far end. Her hair was down and she wore a white galabiya with silver embroidery. I stared; she did not look at me. Standing next to her was a man dressed in a dark grey business suit and wearing a tarbush. They appeared to be talking. He was in his early eighties and bent over with age. I could only see his face in outline; it had craggy, hawk-like features and was pockmarked and dappled but with the frown of unchallenged power. Behind them stood two men in brown suits. Rosemary and Leslie, who had followed my eyes, grabbed my arms and pushed me back into the auditorium. Leslie whispered, "Come on. You'll get in trouble."

In the intervening months, Samira and I were careful to appear noncommittal, rarely looking at each other in class. Samira sometimes called on me to recite; when she did, I was polite but distant. Outside of class, we tried to avoid each other. When we were in the lunchroom, we took precaution to sit on opposite sides. But there was something stronger, an energy like an immense magnetic field; we could not seem to avoid each other. We didn't know where each was, but we always 'knew' in some unspoken way. As Anna, in *The King and I*, put it:

You fly down a street on the chance that you meet
And you meet not really by chance.

But we were not discreet enough.

One morning as I ambled down the hall after a long class with Professor Sakut, Samira stopped me by the fountain with the dragon's head. She had been crying. Her face looked swollen and I thought I saw a bruise on her cheek. Two men in brown suits stood behind her. In a broken voice, she said, "We cannot see each other anymore. They wanted to kill us. They were going to slit your throat and take me into the desert and stone me to death. Nasser intervened." I started forward. She put out her hand. "No, no," she said then turned and walked away. The two men followed her.

About a week later, I went back to the apartment. This time, I went more slowly, paying more attention to my surroundings. The street was lined with rows of mullioned brown buildings; down its centre ran a raised median with tram tracks. There were black light stanchions at intervals and occasional dusty palm trees. I walked past the open doors of small shops, some with striped awnings. There were posters of Nasser everywhere, some new, some tattered; the image of a smiling Nasser was omnipresent, like a force of nature. I continued past vegetable markets, with stacks of fruits and vegetables (and an awful smell of rotting produce) and ducked under overhanging stalks of yellow and black bananas and long gourds of shawarma, covered with flies. Everything I saw seemed tired and dirty.

There was more detail now, but there seemed to be fewer people, fewer women in niqabs. I noticed that most of them were carrying small children who clung to them. It was summer and hot. My shirt stuck, but the atmosphere seemed almost wintry, a lack of human warmth. There seemed to be less noise, less talking, less traffic, as though a soundtrack had been turned down. Something was different, but I couldn't put my finger on it. Trams screeched by. The street seemed much longer, unrolling endlessly; my feet seemed to move much slower.

I arrived at the apartment building and went in. Its marble entrance seemed wider, colder. Then I remembered. The white marble entrance hall was lined with black patterned stripes that I hadn't noticed before. The walls were white marble. I climbed the circular stairs at the back; my footsteps echoed. I stopped on the third-floor landing. The brass-lined cardholder was empty. The apartment seemed deserted. I rang the bell and could hear it echoing inside. No one answered. I picked the lock with the bawab knife, paused, my heart pounding and went in.

The apartment was smaller than I remembered. The brown couch felt hard, the brass-lined bed in the corner had no bedding, and the white dressing table was empty. The striped chair was overturned. The latticed window was covered with dirty brown paper.

There was a faint evanescence of perfume but a stronger feeling of dry silence. The wood floor creaked under me. I looked around. It was only a plain room, with some plain furniture, empty of meaning. I looked around again, one last time and asked myself, *Did this really happen?* The door closed behind me with a final thud.

Occasionally, I thought I saw a black Mercedes 190 drive slowly by the university gate. Sometimes it stopped for a moment. I couldn't see inside it and couldn't tell whether the windshield was cracked.

VI
They Don't See Things the Way We Do

The one good thing about the Garden City House was its view of the Nile. My room happened to directly overlook the Nile; and when I opened the windows, I could feel the weight of the river, sense the wind and energy coming off it, smell its scent and shiver in its cold. From the window, I could see part of the far bank; it was lined with trees and floating restaurants and little houseboats dotted its waterline. Since I was still subject to jet lag and still discombobulated time wise, I would wake up at four in the morning Cairo time.

The second or third morning, I went to the open window and looked out. It was still dark, with maybe a sliver of brightness on the southern horizon. Then, I heard a faint sound coming from the south, from the greyness to my right, down the river, like an echo chamber. The wind blew and the sound swelled. I could make it out as the call to prayer. "Come to prayer. Prayer is better than sleep." It moved toward me down the Nile, moving with the sun, moving from the faraway Sudan toward the city. The words repeated again and again, closer and closer, swelling as they came. Finally, the city erupted in an ear-splitting crescendo: contrapuntal calls to prayer from hundreds of minarets, each with its own variant of sound. The sound had weight of its own, an enormous, physical statement of emotion. The sounds reached an overwhelming volume and then finally trailed off. The city came to life.

Later, I got used to hearing the call to prayer every morning. It became part of the usual noises of the city. I also got used to seeing rows of worshippers praying several times a day; they became a normal background. Some hotel rooms had arrows pointing toward Mecca painted in ceiling corners. Again, in time, these became almost unnoticeable. But all were evidence that I was in the presence of a major and widely practised religion that shaped the way its adherents saw the world.

At Berkeley, I had learned about Islam as a detached scholar, not as an emotionally committed believer. Its starting point was the 'Jahiliyyah' (period of ignorance), a description of pre-Islamic internecine tribal warfare in the Arabian Peninsula: a time characterised by 'barbarism' and 'ignorance', a Hobbesian state of nature on steroids. The solution, as with Hobbes, was to create a community of peace and order. But Hobbes envisioned only a civil society. The Islamic community, the Umma, is a community whose members are joined by a common search for salvation: Islam, the voluntary submission to God. It is a community where peace reigns, a community that is both political and religious, a community that transcends all other communities. The member, the Muslim, is required only to perform five duties: profession of the faith, prayer five times a day, alms giving, pilgrimage to Mecca and fasting. Elegantly simple and emotionally satisfying. Not a surprise, then, that Islam is the world's second largest and fastest growing religion.

The Western Enlightenment represented a fundamental change in the paradigm used to interpret the world. Western 'science' is an alternative to and a competitor with earlier paradigms of understanding. But each paradigm also involves a belief system about the individual self; changing the paradigm of the world means changing the definition of the self. In the West, everybody lucked out; Christianity's 'render unto Caesar' allowed for two competing paradigms to coexist. Not easy (remember Galileo), but it opened the way for social advancements based on hard-nosed research. Baldwin's crusaders and Saladin's Saracens understood each other perfectly. After the Enlightenment, the Middle East and the West increasingly operated in two different realities.

There is only one paradigm in Islam. As a result, Sunni Islamic theologians and scholars (collectively, the 'ulema', or jurists) and just about everybody else have endlessly struggled with the problem of relating Islamic belief with Western science. The Umma is structured by Sharia law, of which four schools (legal systems, really) developed that are followed in different countries. Think of different U.S. state laws. Each school is based on a theory of Quranic interpretation, from strict construction to liberal use of analogy. The issues are the same as those in U.S. constitutional interpretation, and in a sense, the ultimate results in paradigm change are the same.

But it gets more complicated. Arabic is the language of Islam, of God. Were devout Muslims prepared to pollute the language of God with foreign concepts? Watch what you do; words have big time cultural implications. As S. I. Hayakawa pointed out, the medium is the message; change the medium (language) and you change the reality. The Islamic solution has been to move incrementally toward acceptance of the newer paradigm. And considering all the other problems that Muslim countries face, the ulema are moving with resolution and grace. Still, an agonisingly painful adjustment.

In practice, as near as I could tell, the Muslims I knew had exactly the same responses to daily problems that I did. They compartmentalised. They had absolutely no trouble in utilising anything Western science had to offer, from vaccinations to phones. As for polluting the language, they made a very practical use of foreign terms. Enormous common sense. Yet there was a subtle sense of difference that may have been due to my own linguistic problems.

But sometimes the fundamental difference in the way I, as a Westerner, and the Muslims in Cairo saw the world was surprising. In the mornings, after I moved into the apartment, I had taken to reading the 'Egyptian Gazette'. A rag of a paper, but at least it was in English, so I didn't have to keep thumbing through Wehr. One morning, I noticed a small article in the lower right corner of the front page; it stated that the Virgin Mary had been seen in Zeitun. I paid no attention, probably a local rock group. In successive issues, the article got bigger. Finally, there was a story that the Coptic Pope had declared that this was, indeed, the Virgin Mother and that thousands were flocking to see her. I asked Abdul Masih about the story. He said that he had gone to the square where the appearance was happening. "It was the Virgin Mary." He smiled. "I would have recognised her anywhere. Thousands of us saw her."

Broome and Marianne (or Henrietta) went two days before I was to go. But after several Egyptians had been trampled to death by the packed crowds, the government suddenly prohibited all Americans from going. So, I was left only with Broome's account:

The Virgin Mary had originally been seen by a Muslim bus driver who reported a woman in white on top of St Mary's Church late one night. The sightings continued. Coptic authorities investigated; the Vatican sent an emissary. Crowds gathered by the thousands, both Muslims and Christians. Nasser himself attended. After its own investigation, the Egyptian government accepted the vision as true. Broome recounted that when they got there, the square in front of the church was mobbed.

The crowd density was so great that Marianne and other women were picked up off their feet; Broome had to grab her several times to prevent her from being drawn under. Others, he judged from the screams, were not so lucky. After hours of standing, finally, very late at night, they saw something in white appear on the church roof. "So, what was it?" I asked.

"I thought it was a pigeon," Broome replied.

Sociologist Neil Smelser would have analysed this as a classic case of 'collective behaviour': a short-term mass hysteria brought about by large numbers of people closely confined over a long period of time in an emotionally charged atmosphere. But in this case, not so simple: thousands of Egyptians (and visiting officials from the Vatican) saw the Virgin; Broome, the secular American, saw a pigeon. A medieval Christian would have seen the Virgin; a post-Enlightenment 'rational' man would have seen a pigeon.

Who had the better of it, the Egyptians or the American? If it was only a pigeon, the mystery of life would have been lost.

There was another side to Islam. Like any major religion, Islam developed offshoots and splinters, some politicised, some not. And some, like the Muslim Brethren, became mass movements with branches all over the Middle East.

After the Broomes moved out, I would listen to the BBC news on the shortwave radio that I had brought. The early morning news, at about 4:00 a.m. Cairo time, was usually read, or rather croaked, by an ancient announcer. Normally, pretty boring stuff about British and European politics, football scores and the doings of the royals. But this morning, there was something different. "The Israeli forces have invaded Jordan; they have crossed the river near Kharameh," the BBC announcer said. "War, this looks like war. War, war, I say." His words quavered through the static. Very bad news, indeed. I instantly imagined a panicked evacuation. Leaving the kitchen, I went into the bedroom to see what few belongings I might be able to take on short notice. As I reached into the closet, I felt a sudden and painful sting on my right forearm. I looked. I had been stung by a hornet a good two inches long with wide black and yellow stripes: scary. I grabbed Wehr and smashed it. But now, my right arm was swelling. Wonderful, now I would get to run from angry mobs and possibly Israeli troops while losing an arm.

I called the university infirmary. The duty nurse said that the hornet was not dangerous but that its sting was particularly painful and could lead to infection or allergic reaction. She was quite calm; clearly, she had not heard the news. She told me to go to an apothecary (pharmacy) about fifteen blocks away on Qasr Ayni. "They are open all night; I'll call in a prescription for ointment, pain medication and a shot for the allergic reaction. Come back here, and we'll give you the shot," she said.

"Wait a minute," I replied, "that's Muslim Brethren territory, and they won't be friendly."

She tried to reassure me, "Nobody will be up at this hour. Now go."

I left the building and turned down Qasr Ayni; it was still dark and nothing moved. I waked alone, but I seemed to be barely moving, almost standing in place. I knew how the Ancient Mariner must have felt, in a 'painted ship, upon a painted ocean'. I could feel thousands of eyes watching me. After what seemed like a decade, I saw the pharmacy's neon sign and rushed in. The place was warm and filled with boxes and bottles; it seemed comparatively safe. The staff filled the prescriptions. I went back out the door into the dark unknown.

I walked back; the walk seemed longer, the thousand eyes more ominous. No more *Ancient Mariner*, this was now the cornfield in *North by Northwest.* The sky started to lighten, pale fingers of light fanned out from between buildings. Blocks still to go. A splat on the pavement. Then nothing. Then another splat. A rock. I looked back; there was a grey line behind me. I consulted Bond. His answer was immediate: "Run like hell." I did. Or rather, I broke into a lumbering trot, stopping every few yards to catch my breath. Where did all that jogging go? I didn't seem to be moving. It was as though I was on a stationary treadmill; my legs were pumping, but nothing was moving. It was a nightmare.

I could now see the lights of Tahrir Square. I could also see a newsstand and its papers. In red was the word 'HARB'

(War). More splats. Something, probably a rock, actually hit me in the back. The grey line was closer, and one of them was right behind me, reaching out, grabbing my shoulder. I turned, saw wide staring eyes and hit him in the face with the back of my fist. Something crunched, and he went sprawling (my knuckles hurt for a week afterward). I ran across the square, past the black-uniformed traffic policeman. As I passed him, I could see him pulling out his gun. I thought I heard shots behind me as I ran through the university gate. Safe at last.

Not quite. A wall of fear hit me. The courtyard was pandemonium. Groups of students were running aimlessly about; some of the women were crying. All of them seemed to have pocket radios. I shoved my way through to the infirmary, got the shot and pushed back to the department. More panic. Professors were frantically emptying their offices. Staff members were taping windows and carrying sandbags. "The Israelis are coming. The Israelis are coming. They will kill us. They will kill us all!" were the cries I heard.

Hoda appeared out of nowhere. She grabbed me and pushed me into a classroom. The others were there. "We will hide you. Do not fear," she said. "The university is working on a plan to evacuate you by camel train to the Siwa Oasis, and then across Libya to Tunis. Stay here." We sat staring at each other in silence. I could hear the radio blaring in the hall. Suddenly, there was a cheer from outside. I asked Hoda what had happened. "It's the Jordanians. They are holding," she exclaimed. "They are fighting 'with white weapons' (fighting with bravery and honour)." More chatter came from the radio. Then a huge shout from the courtyard. Hoda started crying. "The Israelis are retreating; the Jordanians have held. We are safe." An explosion of car horns erupted from outside.

There was singing and yelling everywhere.

Later that evening, we took taxis across the Nile and then walked as a group to the Opera House for a performance of *Don Giovanni*. The city was all lights. I had never seen it lit up before; I had only seen the constant brownout. The streets were filled with people singing and dancing; the entire city seemed to be in the streets. Car horns were still honking. Everyone smiled and waved at us. Some of them, seeing that we were Americans, handed the women flowers, saying, "*Amerikani; ahlan; ahlan* (welcome; welcome)."

Even the old Opera House seemed to smile. Originally built in late 1869 to celebrate the opening of the canal, as a monument to Khedival cosmopolitanism and in recognition of the large emigre community, the Opera House was a magnificent example of late khedival architecture. 'Aida' was supposed to be performed at its opening, but Verdi hadn't finished it in time, so 'Rigoletto' was performed instead. However, the building had steadily decayed, and was (years later) set on fire by the Brethren. We went in through the ornate lobby and took seats in the rickety upper tier. We were alone except for a small group of 'clappers', young men who had been hired to clap at performances. They clapped vigorously and at random; that night they were especially vigorous. The smell of urine wafted by from the restrooms behind us. But no matter, it was good to be alive and not on the way to the Oasis.

The Italian cast sang with extra enthusiasm; apparently, they were happy to be alive also. After the performance, we all went over to the Garden City House, where the cast was staying, listened to ad hoc arias sung with great enthusiasm, danced (some of the Italian ladies could tango) and got knee-walking drunk.

So who were these Brethren that tried to kill me? (Nothing personal, of course; they just hated foreigners in general.) They were (and are) a millennial movement (not unlike medieval Christian millennials – the Diggers, the Flagellants – or contemporary Jonestown) whose members want to replace an unacceptable present with a millennium in which evil will be abolished. Were they the real face of Islam? From my own experience, emphatically not. They were an attempt to solve a problem that couldn't quickly be solved. The Brethren were founded in 1928 in Ismailia, in the Delta, by Hassan al-Banna (he was assassinated by Egyptian secret police in 1949). Al-Banna, originally a schoolteacher – and that pedigree is important – said that he founded the Brethren because he 'was daily insulted by the activities of British missionaries'. The missionaries were proselytising his students. The core of the Brethren's reason for being was cultural opposition to any introduction of Western practices or values into Egypt, and the corresponding promotion and articulation of Islamic principles. From the beginning, the Brethren were also violently opposed to any form of colonialism.

The Brethren created a sophisticated organisational structure capable of delivering a complete range of social and educational services (including the education of girls and women). Sociologically, the Brethren functioned exactly as political machines did in the U.S.; they mitigated the economic chaos of urbanisation by providing a safety net. But, unlike U.S. machines, they were not corrupt. U.S. machine politicians would not have been welcome in the

Brethren. In 1932, the Brethren moved their headquarters to Cairo: not an accident. Their membership spread all over the Middle East. Officially, the Brethren are reformists, rather than revolutionaries.

However, there is a generation gap between the older leadership, which still believes in peaceful change and a younger faction that espouses jihadism.

The Brethren apparently have a secret military arm (they deny this) that seems to be organised along the cell structure developed by the Assassins (known as the 'Hashshishin' because of their use of hashshish), a schismatic and very fanatical sect in eleventh-century Syria. Parenthetically, the original assassins would have made contemporary ninja warriors look like beginners. No one, not even the best guarded Muslim or Crusader leader was safe. (There is a legend that an assassin got through a row of guards standing to shoulder and into King Richard's tent. The assassin stabbed the king, but the blade was turned by Richard's chain mail. Apparently, Richard regularly slept in his chain mail: good for protection but hard on mistresses. Anyway, I always imagined Richard as looking like George Sanders.) The Brethren's clout rests on its reputation for devotion and honesty. But they are not friendly, and they see Western culture as a threat to the Islamic way of life. In some respects, they are correct.

Brethren membership in many ways was (and is) a microcosm of the larger problem of competing paradigms. Of course, there are alienated young men with no employment opportunities and no real expectations of being taken in by social order perceived as hostile: these make up the cutting edge of social violence everywhere.

But the Brethren recruits in question are those whom sociologists would call the 'transitional' men: individuals who grew up and had their initial identities formed in traditional Muslim families, maybe even families with formal (and traditionally highly valued) Islamic education. But, as they confronted an urbanising society with its changing definition of valuable skills, they were lost, defeated by a vicious acculturation.

The result was predictable: extreme anger at an unjust world and an obsessive clinging to a (now idealised) past. Women, in particular women who appear to have successfully adapted, must be suppressed. The contrast between the woman's 'success' and the man's failure is both too great to bear and a disavowal of the good old days, when the man had great status. I could see these transitional men on the streets; they wore galabiyas with Western jackets over them, not really going anywhere. They lived in rings of tiny, shabby apartments in the inner city.

They were prone to explosive outbursts of mob violence. They were caught between two worlds, with no way out, a film-noir tragedy on a societal scale: a tragedy that generated an ominous threat of unexpected, explosive violence, a tragedy that scared everybody else in Cairo, a tragedy that cut to the heart of the Islamic dilemma.

Hence, not a good idea to walk down Qasr Ayni, away from Tahrir Square and the university.

But there were other aspects of Islam. One quiet Sunday morning, Cohen came over with a bottle of tamarind juice. He demanded to know where the brandy was. I assured him that not only was there excellent vintage brandy (at least six months in cask) but there were also scrambled eggs; I had hired a new cook who could speak both Arabic and some English. We sat down and Cohen, in obvious delight, showed me his latest photos. He was an avid photographer, shooting pictures all over Cairo with a very large camera. Unfortunately, the Egyptian police took umbrage and regularly confiscated his film. They never arrested him, which was odd; they just took the film and handed the camera back.

Cohen handed me the tamarind juice and leaned forward. "I've got something to show you," he gushed.

"More photos?" I asked. "I'm surprised that you have any film left, the way the police keep grabbing it. Let me think, the last time they took your film, you were photographing an 'early Mamluk' building. Very interesting. Right? Except that I've been there and seen the building; there's something that looks like an acquisition antenna behind it and probably a SAM site, hidden away. The Egyptians are very sensitive about their air defence. You lead a charmed life. I don't see why everybody is always complaining about me getting in trouble."

This time, however, Cohen had the goods. The photos were of a Sufi 'dhikr', a ritual during which the faithful work themselves into a state of religious ecstasy to be nearer to God. I leaned forward in astonishment. "How did you get into that?" I asked.

"Sufis are persecuted in Egypt; the Brethren hate them. Those ceremonies are held in secret; you can't just walk in." Cohen grinned. "I have a friend," he explained, "the rest was easy. I put on a galabiya and a skull cap and mumbled."

In Berkeley, I had some academic introduction to Sufism. Its origins were uncertain, possibly Asian, principally Buddhist, with some Hebraic and Christian elements; it was a form of Gnosticism. The Gnostic believes that individual and personal communion with God is possible. Persian, Greek and Roman, Jewish and early Christian sects practised Gnosticism. It has a long tradition. In the contemporary West, Gnostic ideas can be found in a spectrum of writers, from Carl Jung to Madame Blavatsky. Gnosticism, in whatever form, embodies the belief that knowledge of the divine can be experienced directly; that individual union with God is possible without the mediation of religious hierarchies. This charismatic impulse cuts across formal dogma, and because it is so uniquely individualistic, so uncontrollable, so doctrinairely exotic and so schismatic, it has generally been treated as a form of heresy by established religions. Historically, the original charismatic (literally, gift of grace) impulse that animated early Islamic Gnostics became organised (routinized, in Max Weber's usage) into orders, defined systems of doctrine and ritual.

In Egypt, Sufi orders, 'tariqas' (literally, 'paths'), date from the fourteenth century. There are over seventy distinct orders, although believers can belong to more than one, and approximately fifteen per cent of the population practises some form of Sufism. Because Sufism is perceived to be non-political, it is officially tolerated. However, fundamentalist Islamic groups (like the Brethren) have regularly attacked Sufi leaders and desecrated Sufi shrines.

I thumbed through Cohen's photos. They were beautiful. Taken from ground level, they silhouetted the Sufi dancers against a lighted backdrop. Clearly, Cohen had talent. The dancers were frozen in mid-whirl, their robes flying out, their faces filled with rapture. The intensity of their devotion jumped out from the photos. These were images out of time, images that could have been drawn from a nineteenth century print.

All of them that is except the last photo. It was blurred and showed a face with wide eyes and a hand holding a knife. "I take it you had to leave suddenly?" I innocently asked, then, "You're lucky. You could have been an international incident. I can see the headline now: AMERICAN SNOOP KILLED BY MADDENED SUFI DANCERS. Has a nice ring, don't you think?" Cohen lit a Turkish cigarette.

"Never mind that," he growled. "Where's the brandy?" At that point, I heard the noise of horses clopping in the street below.

"Bedouins in Cairo?" I said, in bafflement.

More clopping, but this time I got to the window in time to see. A cavalry detachment, mounted police, passed under the window and turned down the street in front of the building. "I wonder where they're going," I asked myself aloud, then to Cohen, "stay put and enjoy the brandy; I'm going upstairs to look."

I went up the iron stairs and through a green door to the flat roof. There were nine or ten people running frantically from one side to the other. They were Armenians who lived in the building, and they were terrified. They screamed, "It's the Brethren. They're going to kill us all. They're going to kill all the Christians. They're going to burn the city. It's like Black Saturday." Both men and women were crying.

Black Saturday was an apocalyptic event for Cairo. It remains a dark and terrible tale. In 1952, following an armed clash between British police and Egyptian police that left 50 Egyptians dead, the Brethren rampaged in Cairo. Large parts of the city were set on fire; the skyline turned red. Almost a thousand buildings were destroyed; most of downtown Cairo was damaged and looted. Foreigners were hunted down and killed, as were Egyptian Christians. Some British citizens were caught and deliberately burned alive. The British, realising that they could not successfully defend it, prepared to evacuate their embassy. Images of the violence still haunt survivors. There is a saying in Cairo, 'it's a black day', that dates from Black Saturday.

I went to the end of the roof and looked in the direction the Armenians were pointing. At first, I saw nothing, only distant rooflines. But then I heard a low wailing sound, a sound chilling in its eeriness, a sound that seemed to stretch across the horizon. The sound increased. Now I could see puffs of smoke. There were sporadic pistol shots, then heavier shotgun blasts, then the burp, burp, burp of automatic weapons fire. Now lots of smoke. The sound came nearer, down Qasr Ayni toward us, louder and louder. The Armenian women screamed louder and started tearing at their clothes. Finally, the pandemonium reached the corner of the street that fronted our building and turned toward us under the trees. I went back downstairs.

I looked out the dining room window that looked out over the building's front door. In the street below, army trucks had pulled up and soldiers in khaki were climbing out. The soldiers set up a low barricade of sandbags. Two squads clustered around what looked like World War II water-cooled machine guns. They waited.

A line of cavalry in black police uniforms formed in front of the sandbags. On command, they drew wands, like a scene from *Doctor Zhivago*. Their commander trotted forward. He shouted; the wands lowered; the mounted police charged under the trees, horses' hooves skittering on the pavement. There was a tremendous crash. Then riderless horses wandered back. The mob followed, breaking through the sandbags. The machine gunners sprung to their guns and got off a couple of bursts but were quickly overrun as the line of police and horses were pushed back onto the sandbags. The soldiers engaged: a whirling melee of struggling men and arms and legs. Some of the mob headed toward the building door. I could hear the yelling echoing up the stairwell from the lobby.

More trucks arrived. Finally, the soldiers overwhelmed the mob. Men started running back under the trees. The struggle was over in moments. The police and soldiers packed up. Cohen went back to his wife and his apartment.

The next morning, I walked over to Qasr Ayni. The street looked wider, as if a giant bulldozer had rolled down its middle, obliterating everything: curbs, light posts, trees. Only a wide path of brown dust and cement fragments was left. Even the bawabs had disappeared.

For the rest of the day, nothing moved, just silence. Later, Rosemary called to say that there were riots in other parts of the city. The Brethren were targeting anything Western: stores, coffeehouses, nightclubs. The university had called and told her that the staff was planning an evacuation. The speaker said to tell everybody to stay off the streets.

The staff was afraid that it might be another 1952. Rosemary said word was that Nasser was reluctant to order more regular troops into the city because of the possibility of a mutiny. Nasser was scheduled to speak on TV that evening.

Since I had the only TV, everybody – including the wives – came over to watch. Nasser came on; we hunched forward, hoping. He started speaking first in classical Arabic, then he switched to dialect. I had seen him on TV before, confident and charismatic. He once gave an interview to Mike Wallace.

Wallace (questioning): Mr President, I understand that there are Russian Advisors in Egypt.

Nasser (amiably): Wallace (earnestly): Nasser (smiling): Wallace (focussing): Nasser (resigned): Wallace (sternly): Nasser (grinning):

That's true there are Russians.

Do you know how many Russians there are? Of course.

Mr President, can you tell us how many there are? No.

Mr President, why won't you tell us? Because it is a secret.

But not this time. The man on the TV was visibly scared. His eyes were wide. He was sweating. He kept reaching his left hand around to pull at the right side of his neck and collar. The speech was long but not reassuring; he was going to make reforms. We looked at each other. The Siwa Oasis loomed. The rest of the group went home.

The next day, and the next day, again nothing moved. There was only bright, sunlit silence in the square: no traffic, no pedestrians. A few pigeons walked around, pecking at the ground. Some leftover newspapers rolled in the breeze. The morning of the third day was the same: nothing moved. Then, that afternoon, traffic resumed and people appeared. Army units had been ordered in overnight to stop the rioting.

VII
The Thin Red Line and All That

Finally, the end came: older, tired, pounds lighter from bad diet, the 'pharaoh's revenge' and stress, we came together in the department library to plan for our departure. We were badly shaken by the news of Jones's murder. Its violence was an implicit threat to each of us; a threat that had always been there but that had always seemed so very distant. Behind all the banter and bravado was the niggling sense of uncertainty. Everyone asked Rosemary and me what had happened. And we didn't know; all we knew was what we saw.

The last time I had seen Jones alive was about a week before his murder. I had wandered into his office as usual, waved good morning to Saada, and entered. Jones peered at me. "I can tell by your face that you've gone into a guilty mope. Why don't you take up singing? All Welshmen sing; singing makes us happy. Whatever you're thinking, you've got it backwards. Your woman knew exactly what she was doing.

"She probably had her husband's permission. After all, he was an elderly effendi; and in this culture older husbands sometimes allow young wives to have affairs, as long as they are discreet about it. Remember, he had given her everything else she wanted: a TV position, a teaching job. You were perfect, you had no local entanglements, and you were due to leave the country in a year. As you Americans say, 'you were playing in her ball park.'"

Jones leaned back in his chair. "Think of it," he added. "From her point of view, you were actually quite a trophy. You're taller than most, reasonably athletic looking, and you have dark hair with grey at the temples-very much like Nasser himself. You resemble that American movie actor, Widmark (I hated Richard Widmark). Forget all that Orientalist claptrap about the exotic Middle East. You were the exotic one, not her. You were the foreigner. You were the farangi himself, heir to all the misery Westerners have inflicted on the Middle East since the time of the Crusades. The Egyptians have a more developed sense of history than you have. You might not know about the Crusader massacre of the population of Aleppo (about 70,000 people killed), but you can be sure that the Egyptians do. You might as well have a Crusader Cross emblazoned on your shirt."

Then, every inch the professor, he went on, "As far as I am concerned, your pronunciation is barbaric and your grammar atrocious. But you seem to have a certain fluency in the dialect. And I'm told that your command of colloquial insults is impressive. Apparently, you even tried to teach the language lab ladies to tango."

I interjected, "They seemed enthusiastic!" Unfazed, he continued, "These Egyptians are very family oriented and socially conservative. The lab personnel have enough problems supporting their families without your Argentine nonsense. Also, word is that you waggle your index finger at passing buses. I believe you Americans call that, 'giving them the finger—"

I interrupted him, "They started it, and it only happened once."

"Never mind that," he brushed me off. "One day, those buses will stop and the passengers will beat you to death."

"Anyway," he continued grudgingly, "I can see why Egyptian women would find you charming, with a delightful American accent. Their reaction is probably a mixture of attraction and repulsion. Something like that of the Parisian ladies when they first met uncouth American soldiers during World War I. And you told me yourself that even the younger ones, in niqabs, made eyes at you. Didn't you ever stop to think why? You're an exotically handsome stranger to them, that's why. But if you ever stopped to think about it, which you obviously didn't, you would have realised that the Egyptians had as much difficulty relating to you as you did to them."

Jones was annoyingly right. I remembered a conversation I had with Jack about a dinner party he and his wife once attended. (nobody at the university ever invited me to dinner.) Jack said that the host, an administrator, had served whiskey with the main course, instead of wine. Jack thought it odd. But the truth was that the host was not inept; he was simply trying to deal gracefully with a culture that was completely foreign to him.

I thought about it. If we Westerners were guilty of Orientalism, of creating a fictionalised image of the Middle East, were the Middle Easterners creating their own fiction about the West? Call it 'Occidentalism'? Again and again, I was asked about America: what was this strange and wondrous country where men were larger than life and regularly faced down villains in hand-to-hand combat? Where the streets were paved with gold? Where men were always handsome and women were always beautiful? Where everybody lived the good life and nobody seemed to work? All of this was from American films, which were, for most Egyptians, their only source of information. Occidentalism was Hollywood writ large: a conundrum. Robert Burns put it succinctly:

Oh, would some Power give us the gift

To see ourselves as others see us!

It would from many a blunder free us

A burst of noise interrupted my thoughts. The group had moved closer together, almost in a herd instinct, to close ranks, to defend against a foreign, unknowable and hostile environment. Most of us sat at a long mahogany table; some sat in chairs or on sofas; all sat in various attitudes of dejection. The library was silent, almost unfriendly; the books on shelves lining its walls were silent also, just rows of colour and Arabic inscriptions. The wintry sun slanted through the arched windows, its rays cutting diagonal streaks in the papery dust motes that swirled in the air. Outside, the noise of a military parade in the street below periodically seeped through the walls, like the bullring chorus in *Carmen*. Tia got up from her seat on a worn brown leather couch to stand beside me. She touched my arm and said, "Please recite the king's speech. You're always reciting Shakespeare, you love *Henry V*, so that I know that you know it." The rest of the group nodded.

I began:

> My cousin Westmoreland? No, my fair cousin;
> If we are marked to die, we are enow
> To do our country loss; and if to live,
> The fewer men, the greater share of honour.
> [...] Rather proclaim it, Westmoreland, through my host,
> That he which hath no stomach to this fight,
> Let him depart; his passport shall be made,
> And crowns for convoy put into his purse;
> We would not die in that man's company
> That fears his fellowship to die with us.
> [...] From this day to the ending of the world,
> But we in it shall be remembered
> We few, we happy few, we band of brothers

The king's words cracked like pistol shots against the silent, book-bound library walls: words of defiance and assertion, words that split the air at Agincourt and defined who we were. Tia again touched my arm, with a wan 'thank you'. We moved closer together and looked at each other. Just a glance, there were unspoken words, unspoken realisations, unspoken feelings – feelings about something that didn't happen but may never have happened. But too late.

There was more. Even as I uttered the king's words, in my best imitation of Olivier, there remained a question: 'Who are we, and why are we here?' Ostensibly, of course, we were students in an Arabic Studies program. But were we something else? Were we the modern, although lesser, versions of the French scholars that invaded Egypt with Napoleon's troops? Were we academic replacements for 'the thin red line'? How different were we really from the original imperialists? Joseph Schumpeter argues that the imperialists were an out-of-work military class rendered superfluous by the end of feudalism: so much for the viceroys and generals. Michael Fry says that most of the rank-and-file imperialists were really from the Scotch, Irish or Welch underclasses in Victorian Britain. At the bottom of the pecking order, and with little realistic hopes of moving up, these could dramatically change their status by joining the colonial administration or the military. Eventually, these expatriates became a colonial class superimposed on native societies and outspoken in their contempt for the 'natives'. Rudyard Kipling's *The Man Who Would Be King* is an eye-opening portrait of these emigres. Was that vignette so far removed from us?

But we didn't fit either category: no, there was something else. We were obviously not aristocratic warriors (my fencing skills did not qualify), nor were we from an impoverished underclass. There was a different possible interpretation. What I knew of the earlier British (but they could as well have been French or German or Belgian) 'heroes' was that they all had difficult childhoods and exhibited pronounced personality problems.

Burton, who had a harsh Victorian upbringing, was famous for his sudden temper. At 15, he wrote letters to prostitutes; as a student, he challenged other students to duels. Literary rivals crossed him at their peril. Gordon had a similar upbringing; he passed out bibles as calling cards and allegedly molested boys in railway cars. His temper was also explosive. He once declared that he wished he had been born a eunuch; he may have had Asperger's syndrome. Stanley was abandoned by his mother, never knew his father and spent his childhood in an orphan's home. He was often accused of indiscriminate cruelty; he shot people at random. (Even

Gordon, no stranger to violence, thought Stanley was too murderous.) Lawrence's parents were not married; he was a bastard (very bad form in Victorian England). He was always an outsider. While studying at Oxford, he climbed the university's walls (like Bell, who rock climbed) and for a while ate only bananas. After promoting himself through Lowell Thomas, he disappeared in India, disguised as 'Private Shaw'. His final residence, Clouds Hill, was bizarrely furnished: one of the rooms was covered in aluminium foil. He was rumoured to have engaged in self-flagellation. Bell's upbringing was difficult; her mother died when she was a child, and Bell never recovered from the trauma. She developed an almost Freudian relationship with her father. She suffered from severe depression, used drugs and chased (only) married men. Collectively, these men and women were a psychologist's gold mine, and apparently, they all knew each other.

Erik Erikson suggests that such individuals experience 'identity confusion' in adolescence and that sometimes this confusion gets expressed (and maybe resolved) by political activism. Hoffer offers the same analysis but puts it more simply: some political figures suffer from delayed adolescence. But the image of these men and women running around the Middle East like over-age, angst-ridden teenagers playing *Rebel without a Cause* games is too facile.

Social science theory tends toward macro (amalgamate) analysis; it has no alternative. At the micro (individual) level, human beings are unpredictable, because they can think and therefore can change their behaviour. Social science theories are composites of extractions. But the underlying reality is subtle and always changing, a constantly moving reality.

Theories about these 'heroes' are static snapshots. They do not accurately describe individual uniqueness of these individuals which is the task for biographers.

Childhood problems aside, the sweep of their interests and abilities is breath taking. Indiana Jones, the movie scholar-adventurer, is only a pale imitation of these men and women. Their sheer energy and drive were overwhelming; they just never stopped and never gave up. More importantly, all of them were backed by imperial power, a backing that allowed them to project their demons and fantasies onto a world stage.

For example, Bell was by turns a writer (five books), an archaeologist (she helped create the National Museum of Iraq), a political officer (she worked with Lawrence on the Arab Revolt and later peace settlement as well as with British intelligence) and a photographer. Her photographs of the area and its people are hauntingly beautiful.

Her body of photographic work alone would qualify her as one of the great photographers in any generation. Burton, when he wasn't trundling up the Nile, was one of the premier Arabists of his time. He was also very much into pornography: his magisterial, multivolume, translation of *Alf Layla Wa Layla* (A Thousand Nights and a Night) was supplemented by several volumes of idiosyncratic and very kinky notes. *One Thousand and One Nights (The Arabian Nights)* is now known for its genteel Disney renditions of Aladdin, et al. But the original set of eleventh century Abbasid stories was for adults only. It included an extensive how-to sex manual easily equalling the Kama Sutra. The name 'Arabian Nights' means exactly what it says.

The Abbasid elite were extremely cosmopolitan. They had come to power following a massive civil war in the tenth century that involved hundreds of thousands of troops on both sides and which was viciously fought against the original Umayyad dynasty. The Abbasids opened up Islam to all ethnic groups, making it a universal religion, in contrast to the Arab-centric version of the Umayyads. The outcome of the war split Islam into orthodox Sunnis and schismatic Shias. Theologically, the Abbasids were Mutazilites (Rationalists) who applied Greek-style reasoning to theological analysis, a remarkably 'modern' outlook. Intellectually, the Abbasid caliphate is considered to be the 'Golden Age' of Islam, an age of high culture and scholarship. Many of the Greek and Roman classics, which might have been otherwise lost to the West, were translated and preserved by Abbasid scholars.

At night, however, the position of women within the elite was pretty much as described in the *Nights*. There is a tale that a caliph chose two women for his evening; the women were made to sit over a low fire sprinkled with rose petals until they were sufficiently 'perfumed' for the caliph.

There were multiple translations of the *Nights*. The earliest published version was Antoine Galland's romanticised translation. It served as the source for later versions of selected (children's) stories. Galland's version also introduced the character Aladdin (who originally was a Syrian, rather than Abbasid, folklore figure). Then, Edward Lane (Burton's chief Arabist rival) produced a scholarly and relatively sanitised edition. And, of course, finally, there was Burton's porno version. (Lady Burton later published a cleaned-up version as damage control.) Jorge Luis Borges thinks both Lane and Burton produced translations as part of their rivalry: possibly so, but that does not diminish their brilliance. Both Lane and Burton had to have their translations privately published because of the overall salaciousness of the material. One exasperated Victorian commentator observed that Galland was fit for the nursery, Lane was fit for the study, and Burton was fit only for the sewer. By any measure, Burton's translation is clearly a (multivolume) masterpiece.

In the West, the *Arabian Nights*, in all versions – from thrilling adventure stories, to sword-and-sorcery movies starring ex-body builders, to animated cartoons – is considered wonderful entertainment. Its romance has launched careers. But its role in Middle East culture and politics is more problematic; its salacious content caused one country to ban it as offensive to Muslim sensibilities. Ahmed argues that the Abbasid image of women as passive sexual objects, as embodied in the *Nights*, became institutionalised and shaped later Islamic attitudes toward women: oppression and chauvinism. In an irony of history, the original hero, Aladdin, may have been transmuted into the Cairo crotch-grabber.

Even though incredibly talented, most, if not all, of these heroes had a total disregard for their own safety, almost amounting to a death wish, that followed them throughout their careers, in the Middle East and later. Burton went undercover, in peril for his life, investigating the trafficking of women and children in India, then went to Mecca in disguise before travelling to the source of the Nile. After he returned to England, he fought an endless series of duels. Gordon stayed on in Khartoum, refusing to obey direct orders to leave, knowing that staying meant certain death. Even at the end, when the Mahdi's men surrounding him stood back, he charged, firing his pistol. Stanley deliberately confronted, face to face, Tippu Tip, the most murderous slaver in

Zanzibar, a man known for killing people at random. Lawrence, after the Arab Revolt and a sojourn in India, and even though officially retired, raced his motorcycle with abandon over clearly dangerous roads. Bell, who, when younger recklessly climbed rock walls and fell several times (conduct unheard of for a woman in Edwardian England), came back from the desert and finally died at home by a drug overdose.

The words of Saint John Philby who after years of running around the Arabian Peninsula died in bed, succinctly expressed this attitude: "God, I'm bored." The words say volumes. The list could go on forever.

So, the question becomes: how much of this larger-than-life heroic conduct was really a projection of inner turmoil, or a drive for excellence, or a sublimated urge for self-destruction? And how much of it was an affirmation of the human spirit, a zest for adventure? And did this analysis apply to each of us? Were we, in some small way, replicas of these heroes? Or was there another analysis, another explanation? Or were we driven, again in some small way, by the same destructive impulses?

We knew, as a group, that we were going into a post-war chaos. We knew that Egypt was a police state and that Americans would be targeted. Yet we took the obvious risk. Were we then like the Victorian or Edwardian 'heroes'? And did we, like some of them, have what Aristotle would have called the 'hamartia', the tragic flaw; the decisional error that sets in motion a chain of events leading to personal disaster?

Noise from the parade interrupted my thoughts. Bands played, the crowd cheered, units marched. And there was the constant shriek of military jets flying low over the street:

lighter screams from the MIG-19s and 21s, and heavier thunder from the MIG-23s. The building shook and the grim reality of living in a country at war reasserted itself. The 1967 War and the subsequent War of Attrition were always a dark and ominous background to our lives.

When I was between apartments, I spent a few nights at the Garden City House, by now a sort of 'home away from home'. One evening, I went downstairs to dinner on the veranda. The tables, as usual, were mostly empty. But at one, there were three men and one woman. I could hear them talking; they were Americans. They all looked tired and possibly depressed (or at least sour-looking). An odd bunch. I went over and introduced myself.

The woman, who did all the talking (the men sat silent), invited me to join them. I did. She was short, tanned and had a badly sunburned nose, on which she had put some sort of white ointment. She started, and kept, talking, almost a stream of consciousness. The group was part of an archaeological dig in the Valley of the Kings. They had been on station for almost eight months, living at close quarters, under gruelling conditions and (outside of their work) facing utter boredom. Now, they were taking a brief vacation.

The woman (whose name was Eleanor) wouldn't or couldn't stop talking, babbling really; and she kept punctuating her words with spasmodic gestures. "We're playing Agatha Christie games; the new game is called 'kill the director', and we mean to win," she gloated. The men nodded in unison; their expressions never changed; they were like an aging Greek chorus. The woman kept repeating herself and the others kept nodding. Suddenly, she looked up, her eyes wide. "What's that noise? Thunder? I didn't know that Egypt had thunderstorms."

I replied, "No, ma'am, that's artillery fire on the canal. It's not very far from here. There's a war going on." Well, so much for the romance of archaeological digs. I left politely and soon. The artillery barrage continued through most of the night.

In Cairo, I got a first-hand account of what happened in 1967 from McDonald: Nasser had marched his army in broad daylight, flags waving, crowds cheering, down the corniche and across the Qasr al-Nil bridge. "They went right under your windows," he said. Then the army marched into the Sinai to meet its destruction at the Mitla Pass. The 1967 military display was an eerie reprise of the march of Baldwin's crusaders from the gates of Jerusalem to their massacre at the Horns of Hattin in the twelfth century.

The outcome of the war has been well documented by military historians. The Egyptian army took up positions in the Sinai. Nasser blustered. The American government dithered. The world fretted. Finally, the Israelis (correctly) concluded that, if left unanswered, the immediate existential threat would increase and that ultimately Nasserism would destabilise the entire region. They attacked; the Egyptians were caught flat-footed and their air force was destroyed. Deprived of air cover, Egyptian units suffered heavy casualties. They retreated in the open, without air protection, with predictable results. The rest is history.

But in Cairo, there was a different version.

As McDonald related, from the outset the Egyptian mobilisation was a political bluff (although the Egyptian threats seemed real enough to everyone else). The daylight march was aimed as much at a domestic audience, shoring up Nasser's popularity, as it was designed to underscore Nasser's international stature. Even Umm Kalsum was enlisted to sing patriotic songs. But Nasser was a professional military officer and was well aware that his army was no match for the Israelis.

Once his army was in the Sinai, he negotiated a standdown with American Ambassador Talbot. He could win the political battle and cement his role (a role 'in search of a hero', as he put it) as leader of the Arab world with little military risk: his forces could probably hold out for a short time, and the Americans would then bail him out, as they had in 1956. The Americans guaranteed the arrangement, which would give them time to defuse the crisis. Hence, the lack of Egyptian air patrols on the morning of the air attack. (Not that this would have made much difference in the long run.)

The Egyptian Air Force officers believed responsible for this disaster were tried and found guilty and sentenced to long terms. But some of them served these terms under loose house arrest. A number of them were quartered in apartments on the third floor of my building. Occasionally, I would see them out in the street. As it turned out, their sentences were later commuted: an odd leniency given the regime's usual harshness.

The Egyptians were crushed. Not only was their prized military annihilated but their charismatic leader was also discredited and humiliated, and their sense of self-esteem, their 'honour', was destroyed. Cairo was a gloomy place, literally in a state of perpetual brownout. Nasser offered to resign, but he didn't. Egyptians demanded that he stay on as president. But effects of his loss of charisma spread exponentially through Egyptian society in the form of violent and continuing protests.

I had seen the Egyptian army, and I wasn't impressed. At one point, Jack and I were walking along the corniche; the rest were behind us. We were returning from yet another tour. We stopped, our path blocked by a line of dun-coloured military trucks (in the Air Force, I would have called them, 'six-byes'). They were stopped, their engines idling.

Several listless-looking soldiers were slouching around. I noticed that the trucks all seemed to have bald tires. "Your Arabic is better than mine," I said to Jack, "why don't you ask that officer over there (I pointed toward one in a crumpled uniform) why the tires are all bald?" He did (after I elbowed him twice) and then translated the exchange.

"The officer said that they had new tires in warehouses and that, when a war started, they would rush to the warehouses and change tires." What a novel military strategy.

But after about eight months or so, there was what seemed to be a sea change. The Cairenes had cleaned up the streets within a month of our arrival. But they remained visibly dour and sullen. That changed: people began moving about with more briskness; there were more smiles. But there was something else: as Holmes would say, there was clearly 'something afoot'. On the microbuses (small buses with a strictly limited number of passengers), I began to see increasing numbers of young military officers; they all looked like West Point graduates. Around the university, there was talk of large armoured manoeuvres in the Western desert, of full-scale models of Israeli canal fortifications being built, of improved Russian military equipment being delivered. Just talk; maybe just Egyptian wishful thinking.

Professor Khoury had come to Cairo with his family to see what the CASA group was doing. He attended some classes and smiled. I, of course, always managed to be on his left. One afternoon, after another of my dismal performances, I met him in the hall outside class. He was in an uncharacteristic fury. "These Egyptians don't understand traffic rules. They just drive wherever they please, and they don't stop." I asked what happened. He said that the Sunday before, he and his family were driving on the desert highway in a rented VW Beetle. There were lots of tanks on both sides of the highway. All of a sudden, a large tank came out of the desert and hit them. The Beetle rolled, but other than bruises, nobody was hurt. Khoury became apoplectic. "We had the right of way; he should have stopped."

I said, "Look, it sounds like you got hit by a T54. (McDonald had said the Egyptians had begun to receive them.) Those things weigh over thirty tons; your Beetle weighed less than two tons. You could have been killed. What did you expect?" Khoury was not mollified.

"It's the principle of the thing," he grumbled and walked off, fingering his bruises.

Later, Rosemary invited me to a party: the only invitation I ever got. She said that her date was an Egyptian Air Force officer (who, as it turned out, did not look like Omar Sharif) and that he was taking her to a regimental dinner and I could come along. I put on my one sport coat and slacks and went. The regimental mess was packed with uniforms: some fancy, some not. But I noticed that all the officers looked lean and professional. Rosemary pointed out General al-Shazly, the Air Force commander. He looked surprisingly young. After a long series of toasts, which I barely followed, dinner was served. After dinner, drinks and then, like a scene out of *The Four Feathers*, a map of the canal was unrolled. Senior-looking officers started arranging glasses and silverware and talking excitedly. I stayed away from the cluster of officers and couldn't follow most of the conversation, but the gist was obvious.

Later, I asked Rosemary what everybody was saying, but she had been too busy with her date to pay much attention. "That was just man talk." She sniffed. I didn't think so.

I remembered an earlier exchange with Kamel Husayn. He had joined the Nile cruise at Aswan and obviously not just for social purposes. The cruise was to end at the Aswan Dam. It was a huge grey-brown wall, with antlike men and miniature trucks and front-loaders crawling in serpentine lines over its face. There was dust everywhere; rows of klieg lights sent out inverted funnels of dusty light. The air was acrid. The dam was Nasser's answer to Ramses II.

The Egyptians were concerned that foreign intelligence operatives would photograph the dam or even plan its destruction. Hence, Husayn's presence. In any event, unctuous as always, Husayn discoursed on the Aswan Dam, saying that it would be one of the engineering marvels of the world when completed and that it would permit controlled irrigation in the Delta and end the cycle of Nile flooding. But, almost as an aside, he said that, if there was a war, the Egyptians expected the Israelis to use nuclear weapons to destroy the dam and flood the Delta. "In a war," he repeated, "we would be prepared to take over a million casualties." A grim forecast. At the time, I didn't pay much attention.

Another scream from overhead. The crowd noise swelled and seeped through walls; the cheers were a cry of pride and despair. The Egyptians were marching – marching toward a war that they knew they could not win, marching driven by revenge, marching intentionally toward their own destruction.

We finished talking and left the library to go our separate ways. Most of us went home; one of us did not.

Over the months, Leslie and I had become very good friends. Slim, with liquid brown eyes, straight blond hair and a quick, urban savoir-faire, Leslie was more independent than the others. I soon discovered that she had the same crazy sense of humour that I did, the same way of looking at things, and we soon took to having coffee on breaks between classes. (Unhappily, Turkish coffee, but when you're with a charming woman, not so bad.) Unlike the rest of the women, who lived together, Leslie had her own apartment in Bab al-Luq. I never asked, but I sensed that this presented some difficulties as a woman living alone in what was a very macho culture: a culture where we, as foreigners, never quite knew what might happen, a culture in which women were definitely second-class.

Still, I was told, over and over again, that Egyptian women ruled their households and that Egyptian husbands were universally 'henpecked'. I wasn't sure whether I believed all of that, but I thought about the henpecking and wondered how far back this Egyptian tradition might go – perhaps even to pharaonic Egypt?

An image instantly leaped to my mind. Ramses II wearily returns to his private apartment following a long day of planning monuments with his architects. He enters, only to be greeted thus by his consort: "Ramses! Put your hook and sceptre away. If I've told you once, I've told you a thousand times not to leave them lying around. I have enough trouble keeping this palace looking good as it is, without your mess. And do something about that chariot of yours. You're always driving over people, and it's completely filthy." Who knows?

However, it is one thing to 'rule the roost' domestically and another to be seen socially or culturally as an equal. I was told by Hoda that there was a very aggressive 'women's liberation' movement in Cairo: an Egyptian version of the Western suffragettes of the 1900s, a movement that dated from the Wafdist opposition to the khedival government. Egyptian women (veiled) marched for independence along with their male Wafdist counterparts. Later, the founder of the women's rights movement, Hoda Shaarawi (no relation to Hoda), dramatically tore off her veil; other Egyptian women followed.

Egyptian women were ultimately given the right to vote (with restrictions) by the Nasser government in 1956. Other than that, women had limited legal rights and were (and are) not given equal treatment. Hoda said that urban Egyptian women were very militant and continued to demand equality, henpecking or not.

Only twice did I get a hint of the difficulties Leslie faced. One morning, she stormed into class and said, pointing to her shoes, "Look at these; all my clothes have worn out, and now my shoes have fallen apart. Now I have to wear these Egyptian whore shoes (black, low-heeled, sling-back pumps worn by most Egyptian women). All these Egyptian women have legs like Olive Oyl, so it doesn't matter what they wear. It's bad enough that all these guys leer and whistle at me in the street. But I'm expected to look good. It's not fair." She pointed at me. "You, look at you, you can get away with wearing any old clothes. It's outrageous."

Actually, there was a reason for my shabbiness. Before I left, I decided to take only old clothes and a few dress items (in case I was invited to a soiree), on the theory that I might have to leave suddenly. I also kept a small packed suitcase under the bed for a quick getaway. But under the circumstances, it seemed prudent not to argue.

Later, she appeared in tears just before class; her hair was a light green colour. "I ran out of hair colour and had to buy some local stuff, and look what happened," she moaned.

But she was clearly made of sterner stuff and quite resourceful: the whore shoes disappeared, replaced by Eastern European heels; the blond hair returned to its rightful colour. Leslie's self-identity was restored. But unlike the legendary ambassador who had an embassy staff and an Empire to support his foibles, Leslie had to preserve her self-image with very little support. So, who was 'tougher' in insisting on preserving and asserting his or her identity: the ambassador or the student?

There was much more to Leslie than just clothes and hair colour. As it turned out, she was not only an accomplished scholar but an equally accomplished modern dancer in the Martha Graham tradition. She said that she had actually studied with Merce Cunningham. Impressive indeed. But she said that in Cairo there was no place to dance and that she was not only getting physically out of shape but losing her flexibility. Then, one Sunday, she announced that the problem had been solved. She had found a ballet school run by a Ballet Russe prima stranded in Cairo during World War II. She insisted that I come with her to see this miracle.

The school was on the second floor, above an antique shop in an Armenian section of Cairo. One entered through a small door, then up a dark, echoing stairway to a narrow landing. It had a small entry room with several chairs and a table. The studio itself was a larger room with a cracked wooden floor. "Hard on the legs," Leslie said, "but under the circumstances, no matter." The ballet mistress, Madame Zyshova, was an ancient Armenian lady who moved with a grace that belied her obvious age.

She conducted classes with iron discipline, drumming the floor with a short cane and exhorting the class in impatient French, while her assistant pounded out the beat on a dusty upright. The equally ancient barre that ran around all four walls creaked as the students practised four-hundred-year-old figures. Leslie suffered. "That woman is impossible," she once muttered, and after a toe class (only the older girls were allowed to take toe classes), she lamented, "these wood blocks (in the toe shoes) are killing me." And indeed, as I watched her change shoes, I could see the blood and blisters. But she kept on going; I couldn't have done that.

I usually sat in the entry room. The students were mostly girls. The younger ones, about nine to thirteen years old, were dressed in pink tutus with ballet buns, just like their Western counterparts. Leslie and the older girls wore leotards. Usually, the students were accompanied by an adult, a grandparent or relative, who would sit in the anteroom and watch the class. After class, they would critique their charges, demanding to know why the student in question had not done better and complaining loudly that all these lessons were a waste of good money if the student didn't perform as expected. 'Lazy, lazy, lazy,' was a constant refrain.

On the table was a faded picture of Madame Zyshova. Initially, I didn't pay much attention to it, but later, I looked more closely. Obviously taken many years before, it showed a shockingly beautiful woman wearing a white-linen broad-brimmed hat cocked at a jaunty angle, smiling, with flashing eyes and regal posture. Very much the image of a prima ballerina; very much the portrait of someone who could have stepped out of *The Red Shoes*. (I expected Boris Lermontov to walk through the door at any moment.) I pointed the picture out to Leslie and asked her if she could get Madame Zyshova to talk about her past. After a month or so, Leslie returned and recounted her history:

Madame Zyshova had originally studied ballet in Saint Petersburg and then moved to France. She continued studying under the tutelage of prestigious French teachers and finally became a member of the Ballet Russe. There, she worked her way up to principal and at one point had even partnered with Nijinsky himself. Heavy stuff indeed. Imagine dancing with the world's greatest male ballet dancer of the time, performing in productions staged by Diaghilev, with music by Stravinsky, Debussy, Rimsky-Korsakov, with programs illustrated by Picasso and Gris and in costumes and sets by Bakst and Dali. Dali had once designed a set and costumes for the ballet *Rosamunde*; the corps entered the stage through an opening in the stomach of a giant swan; their tights were decorated with colourful lobsters. The audience was not especially thrilled. Parts of the original set are now housed at the University of Tulsa. When asked, Madame Zyshova, unfortunately, did not remember any lobsters. Nevertheless, it was a career 'to die for'.

The partnership did not last long. Zyshova was reassigned to a lesser dancer named Boris. The two eventually married and left Paris for India, just before the Germans marched in.

In Delhi, they opened a nightclub and a ballet school. Boris may not have been a good dancer, but he was a superb businessman. But Zyshova detested India, so the couple moved to Kathmandu, where Boris bought an old palace, renovated it and created the Yak and Yeti Hotel (which still stands). During World War II, Boris distinguished himself as a double agent and creator of chicken a la Kiev. Zyshova, however, had enough and divorced him. She left Nepal and ended up stranded in Cairo during the war. There, she was taken in by the resident Armenian community and remained ever since.

The Armenian community in Cairo was small by the time we arrived. Ethnic Armenians had settled in Egypt as early as the sixth century BC. The Armenians were converted to Christianity by the third century AD. In Egypt, they remained a relatively small population, perhaps 6,000–10,000, until 1915. This number expanded rapidly after 1915, as Armenians fled the Young Turk genocide. Armenian refugees settled in both Cairo and Alexandria (hence Durrell's account). There, they set up small businesses in the inner cities: stores, pawnshops, moneychangers. The population grew between the wars to numbers as high as 40,000. After 1952, the Nasser government enacted 'Socialist Decrees' that discriminated against small businesses in general and Christian-owned businesses in particular. Armenians started emigrating. By the time we arrived in Cairo, there were only 6,000 or so Armenians left, and many of these had moved out of the city proper into its suburbs. The owner of the antique store on the first floor told me that most of his stock came from the estates of Armenians who had fled. I bought a couple of ornate fourteenth-century Quran pages from him.

Madame Zyshova remained in Cairo and taught the children of the Egyptian elites: first the khedival elite and then the Nasserist elite. Although fundamentally different in political outlook, both elites shared a common hunger to be recognised as cosmopolitans, members of the larger (Western) culture. In this case, French culture. French culture was originally imported into Egypt by Napoleon. French occupation forces were accompanied by a small army of scholars and intellectuals. These had some success in indoctrinating their upper-class Egyptian counterparts. (However, they had almost no impact on Muslim non-elites. In fact, the opposite; they generated a backlash against Western culture that ultimately morphed into the Muslim Brethren.) Even after the French were expelled, reformist rulers, beginning with Muhammad Ali, adopted policies of enforced Westernisation (meaning, in practice, 'Frenchification'). The British occupation extended this process: although the occupiers spoke English, the lingua franca was French. Again, this was restricted to the elites and the non-Egyptian, non-Muslim immigrants from other parts of the Middle East that flooded in during the occupation. The Nasserists, while asserting their return to traditional Arab/Muslim values (hence the 'Socialisation Decrees'), simply carried on this tradition, a fact quickly recognised by the Brethren, who became the regime's most implacable enemy.

In this milieu, Madame Zyshova was a carrier of French culture, both the emissary and the repository of a magnificent artistic tradition. She was not just a teacher but an artist in her own right. Mary Pratt would have analysed Madame Zyshova's studio as a contact zone: a social space where competing cultures clash. Pratt would have made this analysis in terms of a colonial relationship. But Madame Zyshova (and the expatriate Armenians in Cairo) were not colonisers, they were refugees. Even more, she was someone who strictly maintained her identity in a very foreign culture.

Madame Zyshova and Leslie hit it off at once; they were very much alike in their passion for dance, and the passion for dance secured their egos. Leslie trained intensely for months under her watchful eye, both of them intensely absorbed and clearly enjoying every minute of it.

But it was not to last. Months later, late one evening, Leslie banged on the apartment door. She looked terrible; her eyes were red, her face was swollen, her hair hung in strings. "Let me in, I need a drink," she said. I did and offered her some Egyptian brandy.

"Here, this tastes like kerosene, but it will do. So, what's going on?" I asked as I watched her collapse on the couch.

"The wife showed up," she whimpered.

"What wife?" I asked, nonplussed.

"Ken's wife, and I didn't even know he was married," she mumbled through the tears. "You know, Ken, the one who's writing his PhD on coin hoards in Yemen. We hit it off as soon as we met. He moved in with me and then, while we were watching an Egyptian movie we knew we were in love. It was wonderful. And then the wife," she moaned. I had no idea. All I knew about Ken was that he was a smallish, nondescript man in his early thirties who never spoke to anyone and apparently never made eye contact with anyone either. I didn't know him, but I didn't like what I saw of him anyway.

I knew a little about coin hoards. Such hoards are a special form of archaeological deposits. Their location and the types of coins found in them can provide the archaeologist with evidence of historical kingdoms and of the trading relationships between these kingdoms. Unlike most archaeological sites, where the artefacts tend to be stratified vertically and provide a chronological, in-depth view, coin hoards provide a lateral, or relational, map of contiguous civilisations. Ancient Yemen was the locus of multiple kingdoms. A highly civilised and prosperous region, it had trade contacts with classical Greece, Rome and even Imperial China and enjoyed agricultural plenty and economic prosperity until the Marib dam, which had stood for centuries, was breached (by rats, according to legend) in the eighth century. The green fields then vanished and the desert took over. Apparently, the universities and private collections in Cairo had caches of Yemeni coins. And that was about all I knew concerning coin hoards in Yemen.

Well, not quite all. There was something else. Leslie's comment about Yemeni coin hoards triggered an earlier memory. One morning before I left for Cairo, as I was walking back through the Berkeley campus after a wretched day of Arabic, I saw what looked like a Lawrence of Arabia poster on a bulletin board outside the student union. I drew nigh: a pasty-faced man with a crooked grin, dressed in full Lawrence gear, complete with dagger, looked back at me. "Who in the hell is that?" I demanded of Brinner when I finally caught him in his office.

"That's the American Lawrence; at least that's what Lowell Thomas says," replied Brinner with a grin. "He's speaking tonight at Dwinelle Hall. You've got to go. I'll be on stage with him."

I did, and when I got there, the place was packed. On the stage was a row of men in chairs; Brinner was at the far end. Front and centre stood the man in the poster, this time in a grey business suit. He announced himself, "I'm Wendell Phillips, and I'm here to tell you about my amazing adventures in Yemen. But first, let me introduce everybody: my mother, Sunshine, who is a gold miner and the motorcycle hill climb champion of Colorado. 'Stand up, Mother." A white-haired lady stood up.

"Next, my new wife, Mona; Mona is the hula hoop champion of Hawaii. Stand up, Mona." A very curvaceous woman with very long brown hair stood up. "Now," he said, "it's not true that I own all of Diamond Head; I just own most of it. And it's also not true that on our wedding night Mona put on boots and kicked me out of bed." Then he went on to introduce his archaeological team, the men on the stage, as 'the greatest this or that in modern archaeology'. Brinner was left out. Finally, another man came onstage and exhorted the audience to clap for 'Wendell Phillips, the world's greatest man'.

I muttered to myself, "I knew it; I knew it." The crowd jumped to its feet, cheering and clapping.

But then, Phillips started the movie of his excavations, and that was an eye-opener. First were camera shots of the Marib dam; it was huge and appeared to stretch from horizon to horizon, much like the Great Wall. I hadn't realised that it was so enormous. Then came pictures of the temple of the Queen of Sheba, an enormous site filled with Greek columns. Then images of gold vessels and statuettes, a hoard resembling a classical Greek version of the King Tut cache. Whatever the hype, Phillips had clearly been on to something.

The next morning, I confronted Brinner. "All right, turn loose, what was all that about?" This time, he had an even broader grin.

"You had better sit down," he said, then went on, "Phillips graduated from Berkeley after the war with a degree in palaeontology, with honours, no less."

I objected, "Wait a minute, Berkeley doesn't have an Archaeology Department; there's no such degree."

Brinner replied, "That's beside the point, but you're getting the idea." Then he continued, "Phillips decided that he wanted to organise archaeological expeditions (he may have wanted to be a new Woolley or Carter), never mind that he had no real training or expertise. Anyway, he organised a 'scholarly' foundation and convinced the CEOs of U.S. Steel, Coca-Cola, Pan Am and Chrysler to bankroll his expeditions. Phillips was the archetype of the travelling salesman; his gift of gab must have been truly impressive. First, he managed to convince the CEOs that he could find the origins of Ali Baba. This didn't work out, but next, he got funding to go after the route of Sinbad the Sailor."

I objected again, "Wait a minute, I'll concede that his expedition to Yemen was real, but the rest was silly. Ali Baba and Sinbad are folk tales."

Brinner intoned, "Listen well, my son, there is more. Phillips was ahead of his time; he hired only beautiful women for his staffers, the original Playboy Bunnies, if you will. One of them was apparently so beautiful that Phillips was worried that she would be kidnapped for a harim."

"Okay, I give up," I said. But Brinner was on a roll. "So, he goes to Yemen and discovers the real thing: a huge hoard of neoclassical artefacts, many of them in solid gold. The problem is that he and his team were little better than looters; they made Carter's people look stodgy by comparison. But he also runs afoul of Imam Yahya, the ruler of Yemen and a very nasty man."

I said, "I've heard of Yahya, a very unpleasant fellow. He used to tie bowstrings around his neck to make his eyes bug out, to look more ferocious. He would kill you as soon as he looked at you."

Brinner agreed, "That's the man.

"Anyway, Phillips had to leave Yemen suddenly – very suddenly. Nonplussed, he went on to become a 'five-percenter'; he negotiated oil concessions for a fee of five percent of the contract price. Of course, he became fantastically rich – he may not have been joking about owning most of Diamond Head."

I shot back, "That's ridiculous!" Brinner laughed.

"What can I say? Welcome to the Middle East. You see, there's hope for you still. Now, go away and clean up your Arabic."

At that point, Leslie interrupted my thoughts by announcing that she was going to kill herself. I assured her that such an idea was nonsense, not believing a word I said. I poured her another drink. Then I sat next to her, holding her hand and feeling overwhelmed and helpless. Her heavy sobs were too powerful for me to respond; after all, I was only a man. Finally, she said that she wanted to go home; I couldn't convince her to stay in the spare bedroom. I half-carried her downstairs to a taxi, rode with her to her apartment, awkwardly rolled her into bed and then left and locked the door behind me, cursing myself as an inept coward for abandoning her. I called Rosemary and told her what had happened. Rosemary said she would help, then added, "You did the right thing."

Leslie didn't show up for class for two days, and when she did, she looked terrible, like a character from *The Lost Weekend*. What had started out as a romantic love affair set to the backdrop of a foreign city, and the acme of an exotic adventure, had for Leslie become a personal tragedy. The Durrell adventure was just that, a romantic story. Like Marius, Leslie discovered that the 'faraway places' were only in her imagination. The same intensity that drove Leslie to Cairo, and that enabled her to survive in a foreign and overtly male-chauvinist culture, had rendered her terribly vulnerable to that most prosaic of American phenomena: the cheating husband. Like Gertrude Bell, Leslie had fallen for a man who was unattainable. The result was a Shakespearean tragedy.

The light went out of her eyes. She stopped her dance classes. I was really never able to connect with her; all I could do was watch her misery. Rosemary said to leave things alone; the women would takeover. "But," she cautioned, "Leslie was an adult; she knew perfectly well what she was getting into; we all told her the guy was no good and that there was something funny going on." Anyway, what was I supposed to do: jump in and rescue her, like some romantic leading man? Become a junior-grade Tyrone Power and make her forget Ken? I dismissed the idea. How outrageous; how egoistic; how utterly male chauvinist. I valued Leslie as a person, and I valued her friendship far too much for any of that nonsense. Nevertheless, I felt helpless and incompetent.

After the rest of us went home, Leslie stayed on in Cairo. But to what point? Later, Brinner told me that she had become more bitter and more withdrawn. The university staff didn't know what to do, so they just let her stay. Finally, the Egyptian police had discovered her in a pool of blood on the floor of her apartment, 'haemorrhaging', as Brinner put it; but he didn't offer any details.

VIII
Ben Gunn's Revenge

At one point, about two-thirds through our stay, a thought came to me: *What if I were Ben Gunn, and stranded in Cairo? What would I miss most?* Ben Gunn craved cheese during his marooning in *Treasure Island*. What would I crave? I had solved the coffee problem. How about pets? The goldfish were a loss, but then I couldn't relate to fish anyway. Besides, I had a real live, if unpleasant, Horus hawk as a sometime substitute. But what else? What about Ben Gunn's cheese? The question sounds simple-minded, but it isn't; self-identity manifests itself in many ways, some complex, some as simple as the desire for a piece of cheese. It isn't the cheese; it's the web of beliefs and relationships that stand behind the cheese. The 'cheese' is just a shorthand expression for a whole cognitive map. Loss of the cheese symbolises the loss of a much larger life experience. Ben Gunn didn't miss 'cheese'; he missed 'home', England. Cheese aside, what would I really miss? The answer came in a flash: hot fudge.

Hot fudge? Now that was bizarre. I had never really thought about hot fudge before. Sure, as a kid I used to love it but as an adult not so much. But now, the craving for hot fudge became an obsession. Like Burton searching for the headwaters of the Nile, I searched Cairo for hot fudge. But, unlike Burton, I did not find my quest. I scoured the local markets without success; all they had were East German chocolates or worse, carob candy. Now carob looked like chocolate but was a disappointing 'wannabe' and definitely not in the same class as hot fudge. What to do: the urge for fudge began to cloud my vision. Instead of concentrating on Arabic syntax in class, I now dreamed of fudge.

Finally, I went to Groppi's, Cairo's iconic chocolate shop and the meeting place for everyone who was anyone: not unlike Duffy's Tavern, 'where the elite meet to eat'. But with a difference: the establishment catered to women and families, unlike the male-only coffeehouses in Cairo. The Cairo Groppi's had been founded in the early 1900s, and everything was top-drawer: opulent furnishings, expensive linens, five-star pastry chefs, and dress code. It was an instant success, and it survived everything. Located in tony Heliopolis, Groppi's had become the 'in' place for expatriates during the occupation. If Groppi's had been located in Alexandria, Durrell's characters would have spent most their time there, sipping tea and philosophising. Actually, the original cafe was opened in Alexandria in the late 1890s, but it quickly closed. Otherwise, the *Quartet* would have become a 'Quintet'.

It had some famous patrons; Lawrence was said to go there almost daily while he was in Cairo. He was often joined there by David Hogarth an archaeologist of note and sometime Keeper of the Ashmolean itself. Hogarth was also a naval intelligence officer. He had promoted Lawrence's early career as a budding archaeologist and then recruited him as an intelligence officer. Apparently, Lawrence and Hogarth planned the Arab Revolt while both were in Cairo. Groppi's may have been the place where the two worked out details over a cup of tea.

Between the wars, Groppi's became not only a high-fashion eatery but the place where royalty, notables and businessmen met to cut deals: an Egyptian version of the Chicago Club. It was also a favourite of secret agents. One British intelligence officer used to treat his German counterparts to a last dessert at Groppi's before arresting them. As the European community grew, Groppi's also became a coffeehouse for intellectuals. The European connection made it also a prime target for anticolonial rage.

Groppi's survived the Muslim Brethren rioting in 1952, and became the darling of the young Nasserists who were the backbone of the new regime At several points, Nasser considered nationalising Groppi's because it was a symbol of Western colonialism, but thought better of it; Groppi's international prestige made it an asset to the regime, and its obvious popularity among his young supporters made it a risky target.

Surely, such a fabled place would have hot fudge by the bucketful. I had only been there a couple of times; the ladies, of course, loved it and went often. When I got there, the place was packed with young Egyptians, all (as near as I could tell) in Western dress: jeans and t-shirts. The crowd looked very European; its members could have been cafe- goers in any cosmopolitan centre: New York, London, Paris, even Tel Aviv. The interior was lined with small square tables, all filled with patrons. What once must have been a magnificent deco interior was now threadbare – paint missing and cracks in the plaster. Nevertheless, the energy was high and the chatter loud. I sat down at the bar and looked down the menu: nothing. Then, I asked a waiter, "Hot fudge?" He had never heard of it. Possibly some strange American dish. Hopes dashed, I left. There was no joy in 'Mudville' and no fudge in Cairo. Fudge would have to wait until I got out of Egypt.

This state of affairs went on for several months without resolution. Finally, the end came; it was time to leave Cairo. I packed and started saying goodbyes. In the meantime, I had to attend a round of farewell social gatherings sponsored by CASA and the university. Some were more interesting than others.

Inji's intense brown eyes fixed on me while her lips pursed with annoyance. Tall, good-looking, with a business-like pageboy and dressed in an haute couture black galabiya and six-inch heels, she was impressive. Inji was the assistant minister of guidance, and as it turned out, she took her job very seriously. We had been invited to a cocktail party given by the university as a last function before we left. Jack and I were standing next to the bar and both of us watched her as she talked with a small group of Egyptians who were clearly deferential. "She must be very important," I muttered.

"She looks scary," Jack replied.

"Well, scary or not, here she comes," I said, because at that moment, one of the Egyptian sycophants had gestured toward us and Inji turned to look. Then she strode toward us, smiling: like an onrushing locomotive. From her expression, I deduced that she must have thought she would just have some light conversation about the government's social policies and perhaps set the bumbling Americans straight, if necessary. As she closed in and held out her right hand with a no-nonsense gesture, I saw the kohl under the dark eyes, the finely drawn features and the high cheekbones: clearly an exotic Arab beauty, and certainly, nobody to be trifled with. With a pang, I also caught the scent of a familiar jasmine perfume.

We chatted formlessly for a few moments while she inquired, in flawless English, how we liked our stay in Egypt. Then Jack (after I elbowed him twice) asked about the Ministry of Guidance. "What are you guiding?" he mused. "Sounds like some sort of propaganda apparatus. We don't have that in America." Inji's eyebrows arched impatiently.

"You don't understand," she snapped back. "We're faced with the problem of moving a backward society into the twentieth century, and we need to control everything to do so. Our population knows nothing. We have to educate the people, and that means we have to tell them what to think."

I gently interjected, "Sounds like thought control." She whipped around to face me.

"If that's what it takes, that's what it takes; the alternative is social chaos. This is not fun and games we're playing."

I suavely changed the subject, like an elegant Charles Boyer soothing an irate Elvira. "We went to the Coptic quarter the other day, and I saw the underground room in the Church of Abu Serga (St Sergius) where the Holy Family is said to have stayed." All smiles now, Inji promptly launched into a description of the Coptic quarter, pointing out that it was originally built on the site of a fifth century BC Roman fort, and that some of the churches date from the fifth century AD. And that, indeed, this may have been the place where baby Moses was placed in a basket.

At that point, I interrupted her by saying that I had also visited the Ben Ezra Synagogue, and that it was surrounded by barbed wire. It was empty, as was the Jewish quarter itself. The only person in the temple was an old, bent-over caretaker who, motioning toward an ancient silver-encased Torah, kept saying, "Touch it, touch it." The silver was badly tarnished. The synagogue echoed; the rows of old wooden chairs sat unused; some of the chairs were overturned.

"What happened to the Jewish community in Cairo?" I asked. The smile vanished.

"There was a war, you know, and the Jews left," she said. "Anyway, we are working on a project to restore the ancient synagogues."

I continued, "But the buildings are empty. I understand that Nasser has expelled the Jews and seized their property. There's no one left." Jack, now sensing a problem, elbowed me gently.

"Just tell it to the Palestinians," Inji shot back, her jaw tightening (actually, rather fetchingly I thought, but this time I was out of range).

At that point, I knew that things might be getting out of control, forget Boyer, and forget Elvira. But I went on anyway (some devil made me do it, maybe the same one that almost got me punched in the Beshtak). "I understand there is a widespread belief that the Virgin Mary is appearing in Zeitun. Apparently, people are getting trampled because of the crowds. Think of the implications; look what happened to the Romans. Why isn't the government taking steps to deal with this?" I looked concerned. This last was just too much.

"Look, mister," she snarled, now in Arabic, "the Egyptian government has quite enough trouble with the Israeli army as it is, without taking on the Virgin Mary in addition." With that, she spun around and walked away, her stilettos clicking angrily on the tiles.

Jack looked at me unhappily. "You know, you really are going to get us killed. The Arab woman was bad enough, but then you knock down Nasser's daughter in the school library."

I objected, "Wait a minute, she tripped over her own feet. Besides, I helped her up like a gentleman."

Jack replied morosely, "That's not the way I heard it. And you were lucky there was no security. But now you infuriate the number two in the ministry of truth. Think where you are. That woman can make us disappear."

I responded, "Not with two weeks to go. Anyway, she had all the charm of a snake. And never mind baby Moses. Back to the bar; they're actually serving American bourbon."

The parties ended; the farewells were said: a sense of loss was all that was left. I was the last to leave; the others had already taken flights to different destinations and Leslie was nowhere to be found. I looked around the empty apartment. I went back to the old classrooms. I could hear in my mind the echoes of talk and laughter, of stress and fear. I could see vague images of translucent faces and gestures, faint flickers of smiles. But now there was only silence and emptiness; now only rooms with no meaning, just chairs and tables.

When I got to the airport, I again looked around; this time, it seemed different. True, the gun emplacements were still visible, but clearly, the scene had changed. There were airplanes on the tarmac and the terminal was brighter. The tape and sandbags were gone; the glass doors were clear of dust. The interior hallways were clean; the tile floors were shiny; the counters were open. There were people everywhere, walking around, smiling and conversing in burbling Arabic. Also, oddly, everything seemed smaller.

Either that or I was bigger. Like Alice, who kept changing sizes, I experienced an environment wherein I kept changing. Strange, the more uncertain I felt, the larger the rest of the world looked, not necessarily threatening, just larger. But now, it was the reverse; I felt very large, even massive, and the world around me seemed smaller.

At first glance, the adventures of Dorothy and Alice seem to parallel. But not so, Dorothy clearly was physically in an alternate universe. Not so Alice. Wonderland may have been the 'real' world seen through the lens of her mind's eye (or cognitive screen, which is a 'looking glass'): hence the sometimes Freudian interpretations of the book.

The alternate universe for Alice was an internal one: something like the 'reality' experienced by those with clinically diagnosed schizophrenia. But in Alice's case, it was entirely normal and more likely driven by a lively imagination. As Alice changes and grows up, she sees not herself but the world around her changing in size and shape.

Massive or not, I still had to go through Egyptian customs and get on the plane. On the flight stopovers, I tried again to find some hot fudge. Maybe that would fill the emptiness.

The first stop was Beirut, which had whiskey and American professional wrestling, but no fudge. I had been to Beirut years before, as part of the American invasion force in 1958: Beirut was the capital of a French Mandate carved out of Muslim Syria in 1920 to protect its majority Christian community. The French considered Lebanon a special protectorate and worked to install French culture there. French became Lebanon's second language and was mandatory in grade schools. Beirut became the Paris of the Middle East and deservedly so: its architecture was a unique blend of French and Ottoman styles. Its culture was a cosmopolitan blend of French and Arab cultures: intense intellectual activity, high fashion and very advanced views on women's rights. The young singer Fayruz got her start in Beirut and went on to become not only the 'First Lady of Lebanese Singing' but an international singing star as well. It was said that any Parisian would instantly feel at home in Beirut.

When I landed and went into the airport terminal, I could immediately feel the ebullience of the city: on the walls were large displays that showed fluctuations in exchange rates and local stock prices. The terminal looked like a cross between the New York Stock Exchange and a Las Vegas betting parlour. It was packed with travellers obviously coming from the Middle East and the rest of the world.

I took a cab, rather than military transportation. The driver spoke flawless English (and probably several other languages). When we got to the city, I noticed that most buildings had cranes on top. I asked the driver. He laughed and said, "Beirut is the only city where streets are considered to be in the way of tall buildings. The reason that there are cranes is because their owners never know when they might want to add another storey."

Then I asked, "Do they still have nude beaches?" More laughter.

"Yes, but you can't get in; better you should look at the Cedars of Lebanon." I stayed in the Le Bristol and spent the few days shopping (the sectarian war seemed to be conducted outside of business hours) and the nights watching belly dancers in the hotel's 'Casbah'. Not bad for a young lieutenant.

Ten years later, the atmosphere was very different. Georg Simmel wrote that opponents in a protracted conflict tend to be organised in mirror images and to develop tacitly shared rules of engagement. Think of the Hague Conventions. Think of the national security structures of the U.S. and U.S.S.R. during the Cold War. But not so in Lebanon, rather the reverse. The sectarian conflict, and now the added Palestinian-Israeli violence, had metastasized through Beirut and Southern Lebanon. Any restraints on the random violence seemed to have disappeared. I did not see any checkpoints, but I was told that there were many in the outskirts of the city. The brutality of the violence seemed to have increased exponentially. Lebanon was descending into a Middle Eastern version of *Lord of the Flies.*

At one of the last farewell parties in Cairo, I talked with Malcom Kerr. Born and brought up in Lebanon, with Beirut as a second home, Kerr had become a well-respected Middle East scholar. I had known him as a sunny and optimistic person, dedicated to his scholarship. But at the party, he seemed worried, even grim. He said that he had been offered the presidency of the American University of Beirut, Cairo's sister university. He was debating whether to accept but was concerned for his and his family's safety. Ultimately, he did accept. And then, one morning, two gunmen shot him just outside his office. It was rumoured that one of the gunmen tried to lap up the blood.

I stayed in Beirut only a few days: just long enough to decompress from living in Cairo. While I was there, I was told to be very cautious about leaving the hotel: random shootings and kidnappings had become daily events. When I got into the taxi to drive to the airport, I sighed with relief. The Israelis bombed the airport shortly after I flew out.

Years later, I saw TV pictures of the aftermath of the Christian Phalangist attack on the PLO camps at Sabra and Shatila. The PLO fighters, forewarned, had fled, leaving only unarmed women and children. The Phalangists massacred them all – between 800 and 3,500 victims – and then stacked them in mounds. The TV zeroed in on one mound of bodies: in front was a girl, maybe ten years old, in a blue gingham dress, eyes wide open, staring, with a teddy bear clutched in her left arm. Hulagu Khan, whose forces massacred most of the population of Baghdad (some 90,000 people) in the thirteenth century and cemented hundreds alive inside walls, would have smiled in recognition.

But that was later.

Then off to Istanbul. Surely, in the sometime capital of a thousand-year-old empire, there would be fudge. I stayed at the Hilton; its dining room was marvellous. It had ornate walnut panelling, starched white linens, uniformed waiters and even monocle-wearing German patrons, looking like leftovers from World War I. I felt that I had been transported in time to 1915. But still no fudge.

I went to all the tourist sites. First, I went to Topkapi Palace, the original seat of the Ottoman sultans since the fifteenth century. It was a magnificent complex; its opulent chambers were covered with blue and white tiles with Arabic calligraphy. Its walls, with alternating filigreed arches, glittered with ornate gold designs; it was easily as opulent as any of Ludwig's castles. I saw the robe and sword of the Prophet. I also saw a set of porcelain dishes, a gift from the emperor of China, that were designed to crack if poisoned food was placed on them: a hint of the deadly nature of palace politics.

Surprisingly, I found that I could read the Arabic inscriptions on the walls; it was easy. Later, at the Hagia Sophia, I read aloud the Quranic verses on plaques high up in the arches, much like Jones had done months before. The Turkish tour guide was annoyed, to say the least. In 1928, Ataturk decreed that only Turkish could be taught in schools, a version of the Latin alphabet was introduced to replace the older Arabic script. The tour guide could not read Arabic. She was cut off from her past; her loss was incalculable.

I went to the Grand Bazaar: Kapalicarsi. Founded in the fifteenth century, it was originally part of a complex that included a slave market (depicted in numerous Orientalist paintings). Unlike the older Egyptian Khan, which is open-air, Kapalicarsi is covered; it resembles an enclosed shopping mall. It is enormous; its hallways glitter; its shops are 'modern'. I strolled along, in wonder, like any tourist, until I found a carpet dealer's shop. I went in through the glass door.

The dealer greeted me warmly and asked if I would like a Coke. I would. He closed the glass door, and with a flourish, began displaying his rugs. I asked to see small Kayseri rugs, something I could carry onto the plane. Kayseri rugs were (and still are) made in the town of Kayseri, which was at one time on the Silk Route. The rugs have Asian and Iranian design elements, many of them featuring vine-like floral patterns. Silk versions are used as tapestries. He showed me several rugs. I picked out a red one and examined it with exaggerated care. "It has a flaw," I said, disappointed.

"No, no, it is not a flaw," he responded. "Only God makes perfection."

He went on, "The rug is 200 lira, but I'm going to do something crazy, just for you. I'll give it to you for 100 lira." (Aha, the price is flexible.) He watched as a group of tourists passed the glass door. I smiled in appreciation and opened my wallet, fingering the bills.

"But I have only 50 lira; perhaps we should look at something else." Another tourist group passed. He looked concerned; potential customers were passing the closed door. I followed his eyes. (Aha, there is leverage.) "Well, I don't know where I can get the extra cash," I mused. "Perhaps another Coke." Another group passed while I sat smiling.

"All right, all right, you can have it for 50 lira," he said. I fingered the bills. "But wait, if I give you 50 lira, then I won't have any money left for the bus." (Abe Cohen would have called this, 'sweetening the deal')

The dealer shoved the now folded up rug at me and snarled, "Just give me 40 lira and please leave." I did. But as I left, I thought to myself, this negotiation was easier than what I had to do almost every day in Cairo.

I had become another (younger) Father William:

"You are old," said the youth, "and your jaws are too weak For anything tougher than suet.

"Yet you finished the goose, with the bones and the beak—Pray, how did you manage to do it?"

"In my youth," said his father, "I took to the law, And argued each case with my wife.

"And the muscular strength, which it gave to my jaw, Has lasted the rest of my life."

There is a cautionary tale about a youth who went to a Tibetan monastery to become strong. After months of doing the same tasks, nothing seemed to change. He didn't realise his prodigious strength until he left the monastery and returned to the everyday world. As with the youth, when we change, the change is gradual and continuous, and we don't realise what is happening. It is only when we come up against the external world that we discover the change. Perhaps in the year in Egypt I had become more Egyptian than I knew.

But the quest was not yet hopeless; there was still London. London had Wimpy's, home of the (British) hamburger; clearly, Wimpy's would have fudge. After all, Wimpy's bore the name of the character in Popeye who mooched hamburgers and was famous for the offer: "I'll gladly pay you Tuesday for a hamburger today." But, like the original Wimpy, who never returned on Tuesday, Wimpy's the restaurant did not produce the goods either: chocolate syrup by the (British) gallon, yes, but no fudge.

I could sense Ben Gunn's delight. This was rapidly becoming a matter of life and death: curious, how such a seemingly inconsequential wish should suddenly become so important. It was now obvious why Dorothy obsessed over the Ruby Slippers.

While in London, I visited the British Museum and walked through the galleries. The Greek and Roman exhibits were a delight: filled with marble statues of incredible, even breath-taking beauty. Imagine the skill, the knowledge of human anatomy, the precision and control and the conceptual power of a Praxiteles who could take unformed rock and turn it into a lifelike statue. Just standing in front of these pieces and realising that they were originally formless marble slabs boggled my mind.

Then I went to the Egyptian collection. I admired the Rosetta stone and the massive head of Ramses II (clearly up to his public relations standards). British colonial acquisition of this bust was the impetus for building the rest of the Egyptian collection. But then I had a strange, unexpected experience while I watched the crowds of tourists gawking at statues of Egyptian pharaohs. Obviously, they were observing something foreign, something even slightly repellent. To me, these pharaohs were very familiar, like old friends. I had seen them almost on a daily basis, and I remembered once when they had looked down on me, in another museum, a hundred years before.

I flew back on TWA 147. The plane looked the same as before, maybe slightly more worn. As I settled into a seat clearly designed for midgets and the stewardess served me a glass of real French wine, I reflected. "Where do I begin?" I asked myself.

"You must begin at the beginning," the Red Queen replied.

"So, do I start with Durrell or Woody Allen?" I asked again.

"Just start with both and get on with it," said Bond.

Woody Allen argues that we live in two worlds: the world we actually deal with every day and the world of our imagination, a world of our dreams, a 'golden era'. When we signed on to CASA, we all thought that we were about to enter that 'golden era', however each of us imagined it some imaginings were drawn from literature, like the *Quartet*, and for some of us Cairo was to be the scene of a 'real' Durrell romantic fantasy. For others, the imaginings were composites of old movies and adventure novels (like my own fantasies). But the imagination was not the reality, as we quickly found out. The perfect 'golden era' existed only in our minds; the actual 'golden era' we had to live in was an imperfect imitation, a second or third order of reality, as Aristotle would have put it. So, each of us created our own reality: a composite of realities 'real' or imagined.

A psychologist would describe this as a form of 'socio emotive selectivity', meaning that we tend to remember only positive experiences. The 'Golden Age' or the nostalgic 'Good Old Days' are also the 'Bad Old Days' in reality. But the concept of a 'Golden Age' is much more than a faulty remembrance; it provides a benchmark by which to judge the present and a goal worth striving for. Golden Ages may look to the past, but they are also aspirations for the future.

There are two realities: an inner reality (the self-image) and an outer one (the environment); the interplay between the two depends on the individual. For the Victorian or Edwardian 'heroes', the interplay was determined by some childhood trauma that shaped their self-image and drove them into ferocious action.

For us, each handled the interplay in his or her own way. Jack saw Cairo through the eyes of a scholar; for him, it was a chance to see history close up. Mark remained an enigma; he was always nervous in class, and his hands trembled; I suspected something, but I never asked. Nora, who could easily deal with contemporary Cairo was happier in its pharaonic past. Broome perceived everything as a potential moneymaking opportunity. Rosemary just bubbled with life; to her, everything was new and interesting. Tia, wounded, adopted the wary alertness of a professional soldier, a wariness that choked her. Cohen saw the world through the lens of a camera; in a way, he was a recreation of another photographer, Bell, from sixty years earlier. Leslie strove impetuously to make her golden era a reality and that striving cost her terribly. I escaped into a world of fantasy; when the 'real' world became too grim, I went back in time, to an earlier (often imaginary) era (in glorious Technicolor), or to a world of pure fantasy.

But we all came back changed in some fundamental way. In an allegorical sense, all of us had drunk of the waters and were 'forever condemned to return'. Our experiences in Cairo had changed us and would remain 'forever' a permanent part of our identity.

The stage on which we played also changed. Cairo in the sixties was, for later Egyptian literati, seen in its own right as the golden age of Egyptian artistic and intellectual achievement. It was the locus of a glittering cinema, a robust and elegant literary life, an artistic flowering and a cosmopolitan outlook. The Khedival drive to make Cairo a physical Paris was complemented by a Cairene elite who made the city an intellectual Paris as well. Durrell's emigre community would have been (and still may be) at home in the Cairo of the 'sixties'; but the Cairo of the 'sixties' was an indigenous creation.

In a curious way, the Egyptian writers and artists who produced this golden age also produced their own Orientalist vision. The image that comes through in their works (with some notable exceptions) is that of an idealised history. Idealised in the sense that its elements are abstracted from an underlying, and far more complex, reality. Like the Western social scientists, the Egyptians were creating their own models.

But there was a profound counterthrust: the older Islamic society asserted itself with a vengeance following the Six-Day War. The trauma of defeat opened the way for the Brethren. It is no accident that the principal targets of Brethren violence were Western-appearing edifices: stores, restaurants and hotels, even tourist buses: but especially, nightclubs. Nightclubs, which the elite saw as examples of Western cosmopolitanism and sophistication, were seen by the Brethren as examples of Western decadence and domination and were regularly targeted.

These implacable enemies shared an identical viewpoint, just as their medieval Christian and Muslim counter parts centuries before did. Both were correct but for different reasons. To use Pratt's term, Egyptian nightclubs were contact zones where Egyptian Western and Islamic cultures met. Even the belly dancing was a cultural microcosm of this contact: Samia Gamal (like her counterpart Serena Wilson) had been influenced by the American Ruth Saint Denis, who transformed the Egyptian 'raqs baladi' into the more international 'raqs sharqi' (Oriental dance). The hotels, restaurants and casinos that housed these dancers were themselves blends of Egyptian and Beaux Arts styles. But where the Cairo elite saw this as progress, the Islamicists saw it as a Western attack on Islamic values. Both sides were right.

These competing realities may synthesise in time. Hopefully for the Egyptians, they may yet create their own truly authentic 'Egyptian Revival'; a revival that blends the best elements of both Western and Islamic culture and that meshes personal stability with personal growth. Hegel may yet smile.

The plane bumped and then smoothed out. I dozed off.

Finally, the plane landed at La Guardia. I ran through customs like an old alcoholic, unshaven, in a tattered white suit, desperately crawling toward the lights of a welcoming bar in the distance. The immigration officer looked at my passport with its Egyptian stamps and frowned. Then he looked up with a smile and said, "Welcome home." I left customs and raced down the terminal walkway. It was an elongated blur of shops – newspaper stores, bookstores, liquor stores – all with neon signs endlessly beckoning. I zigzagged back and forth in my hurry. At last a hamburger joint. I staggered to the counter.

"Have you got hot fudge sundaes," I pleaded.

"Yes, we do." The counter lady smiled.

"I'll take two, heavy on the fudge and hurry," I croaked. The sundaes came; I took a spoonful.

Home at last.

Epilogue

After our tour of the Tut exhibits, Melisande and I strolled through the various art exhibits and then went to the coffee lounge. There, we spent a few moments discussing what we'd seen. Melisande complained that modern art had declined. "Art should be uplifting as well as functional. There's nothing uplifting or functional about sculptures made of rusty plumbing."

I replied, "Your nostalgia for a past golden age has got the better of you. The rusty plumbing you saw is now considered to have a message. You're not supposed to like it or be uplifted. You're supposed to be instructed."

Then, changing the subject I said, "How is your sister, Celeste?" Unlike Melisande, who was cool and reserved, Celeste was ebullient and supremely confident. She was currently a professor of Medieval English at a Los Angeles university and a very good structural linguist with a burgeoning international reputation. She was also a professor by day and a ballet teacher by night. Melisande thought a moment.

"She's gone off to Peru. Every year, she goes to Peru or Uruguay or someplace, to teach English in some village. She's fluent in Spanish and also in a couple of Indian dialects.

She brings back pre-Columbian artefacts; I don't know how she gets them."

I interjected, "Wait, does she have a large purse?" Melisande laughed.

"No, Dad. Anyway, that is so old-fashioned; she uses a really big backpack." I leaned back, admonished in my old age. Melisande continued, "She's like you, Dad, always going off to some godforsaken place."

We finished our coffee and left.

CPSIA information can be obtained
at www.ICGtesting.com
Printed in the USA
LVHW020402260422
717134LV00012B/358